STRATEGIC NEGOTIATION

A Breakthrough 4-Step Process for Effective Business Negotiation

Brian J. Dietmeyer with Rob Kaplan

Dearborn™
Trade Publishing
A **Kaplan Professional** Company

Vice President and Publisher: Cynthia A. Zigmund
Acquisitions Editor: Michael Cunningham
Senior Managing Editor: Jack Kiburz
Interior Design: Lucy Jenkins
Cover Design: Scott Rattray, Rattray Design
Typesetting: the dotted i

Think! Inc. is a global negotiation consultancy offering a wide range of services from instructor-led or Web-based Strategic Negotiation workshops to implemented organizational solutions. Think! Inc. was founded by Max Bazerman, Ph.D., author of *Negotiating Rationally* and a professor at the Harvard Business School. 312.850.1190

Published by Dearborn Trade Publishing
A Kaplan Professional Company

Printed in the United States of America

04   05   06   07   10 9 8 7 6 5 4 3 2 1

Library of Congress Cataloging-in-Publication Data

Dietmeyer, Brian J.
    Strategic negotiation : a breakthrough process for effective business negotiation / Brian J. Dietmeyer with Rob Kaplan ; foreword by Max H. Bazerman.
        p.   cm.
    Includes index.
    ISBN 0-7931-8304-9 (6x9 hardcover)
    1. Negotiation in business.   I. Kaplan, Rob.   II. Title.
HD58.6.D543 2003
658.4'052—dc22

2003027374

ADVANCE PRAISE FOR *STRATEGIC NEGOTIATION*

"In *Strategic Negotiation,* Brian Dietmeyer offers commonsense principles and strategies that, when applied to the field of business negotiation, will revolutionize the process as you know it. This book will add immeasurable value to any negotiation!"

Anthony Robbins, Author, *Awaken the Giant Within* and *Unlimited Power*

"Finally a book on commonsense negotiation. No gimmicks, no tactics, no games—just rational decision making grounded in a bone-deep understanding of both sides. This dynamic process is the only one I have seen that allows for a total integration into the organizational culture. Now that is impact."

Paul Ruane, Director of Sales Training, Schering-Plough Health Care Products

"What's so great about this book is that the authors are not only great negotiators, they are also great teachers. You'll learn how to leverage information, how to construct a powerful negotiation process, and how to apply superior skills to achieve spectacular outcomes. This book is truly illuminating from cover to cover."

Gerhard Gschwandtner, Founder and Publisher, *Selling Power Magazine*

"The Microsoft Business Solutions sales team has used the Strategic Negotiation process for four years. This process has been extremely effective in teaching our sales force as well as our certified account executives. We praise Brian and Rob for creating a successful process that truly stands the test of time."

Robert Deshaies, Regional Vice President, Microsoft Business Solutions

"Dietmeyer and Kaplan have written a must-read book that takes what many consider an art form and demystifies it into an easily understandable process."

Don Sterkel, President, Society for Sales and Marketing Training Professionals, and Senior Director, Learning and Development, Time Warner Retail

"The Strategic Negotiation process and supporting principles are guiding us to better value-based solutions for our customers and for us."

Bill Bosworth, Organizational Development Director, National Sales, Coca-Cola Enterprises

"*Strategic Negotiation* is a must-read for salespeople and sales leaders. It creates a roadmap for a new and constructive approach to creating value in customer negotiation without sacrificing company profit."

Roger Dow, Senior Vice President, Global and Field Sales, Marriott International Inc.

"Every day the gap between transactional deals and strategic deals is widening, with transactional deals being reduced to online auctions and strategic deals taking on the characteristics of joint ventures. It's imperative that deal makers continue to evolve not only in relation to their general management skills but also in their negotiating process. *Strategic Negotiation* excellently outlines a process that today's negotiators can use to understand the game of three-dimensional 'chess' they must play to be successful."

Ken Redding, Vice President, Strategic Business Development, Starbucks

"*Strategic Negotiation* provides a process-driven framework, specific principles, and functional worksheets to effectively negotiate capital expenditures. This book will be an indispensable source of guidance for sellers that all readers will appreciate and reference during contract negotiations."

Kevin Larson, Vice President, Chief Information Officer, AAR Corporation

"Successfully negotiating development agreements is the keystone to establishing long-term, mutually beneficial relationships with our franchisees. As a real-world practitioner, I look for any edge that will help me negotiate the best agreements possible. *Strategic Negotiation* absolutely provides that edge. This isn't ivory tower theory, but a relevant, applicable approach to the negotiation process."

Peter Wright, Director of Franchising, Panera Bread

"Before the Think! Inc. negotiation process, the worst situation was not losing a deal, it was winning a deal, and then hearing from our internal partners it was a 'bad' deal. Today our negotiations are rational and when we complete a deal everyone supports it and understands its value."

David Lipps, Senior Vice President, Aegon DMS

"*Strategic Negotiation* is a key part of our sales process that can help us close more business, and create added value that can be shared with our customers for mutual benefit."

Russ Weisz, Vice President, Worldwide Sales Operations, KLA Tencor

"Traditional negotiation handbooks focus on the skills of the individual negotiator. But while these are important, it is their combination with organizational competence that is critical. Superior negotiated outcomes are not a matter of luck; they come from a well-defined and managed process. There is no doubt in my mind that Think! Inc. is a leader in this area, and you may well hope that your competitors are not reading this book!"

Tim Cummins, Executive Director, International Association of Contract and Commercial Managers

"The strength and trust in a business relationship is usually revealed in the negotiation process. *Strategic Negotiation* is a guide leading to a value-based, long-term relationship."

John Dale, Vice President, Feed Additives–North America, Degussa

"In a climate of increasing commoditization, the negotiating process is often compromised by salespeople tactically reacting to customer pressure around pricing. This book provides a roadmap to adopting negotiating strategies that complement overall account management strategy, enabling greater success in the present that also preserves the long-term objectives for the account."

Lisa Napolitano, President and CEO, Strategic Account Management Association

"The most critical step in valuable business growth is successful negotiations. Regardless of the business need, *Strategic Negotiation* offers a compelling process to ensure every negotiation maximizes the opportunity for value creation. For the entire sales, account management, and executive teams, investing the time and effort to adopt Brian Dietmeyer's tested and proven process will pay tremendous dividends!"

Jim Luce, Chief Marketing Officer, Biogentec

"The negotiating process provided in *Strategic Negotiation* provides an invaluable structure, moving a sales force toward conscious competence while maximizing a product or service's value and indirectly maintaining market integrity. By proactively analyzing all functions of the negotiation, the result is a mature, disciplined approach to growing sales and market share."

John Akers, Director, Management Development, Guidant

DEDICATION

To my business partner and friend, Max Bazerman—the book doesn't exist without you. Mom, Dad, John, Joanne, Dan, Sandy, Nancy, Chad, Renee, Cassidi, Brianna, Dylan, Lauren, Elise, Denise, and Brent—I love you. My associates at Think!—I appreciate you more than you know.

BJD

To the memory of Arnie Krigel, who would have liked it.

RAK

C o n t e n t s

PART THREE

Applying the Process

The past 25 years have been an exciting time in the field of negotiation. We moved past the era of "win-lose" negotiations training and beyond the simplicity of "win-win" messages. Leading thinkers in negotiation now realize that it is critical to think simultaneously about creating value and claiming your share. Fortunately, new writing leads us toward logical strategies and process, and *Strategic Negotiation* is an important part of that movement.

As the coauthor (with Margaret Neale) of *Negotiating Rationally*, I have been fascinated with exploring the question of how to help professionals make wiser decisions in negotiations. My applied work has attempted to take the current state of research and bring it into a useful format for managers. In 1996, Brian Dietmeyer left his position as vice president of sales at Marriott and took the lead in creating a new training firm, Think Inc.! I am proud to be a part of Think Inc.!

Strategic Negotiation brings Brian's efforts from Think Inc.! to a broader audience. It is based on fascinating new research in the field of negotiation, some of it covered in *Negotiating Rationally* and some developed in the decade since the publication of that book. At the same time, *Strategic Negotiation* adds the experience Brian brought from Marriott and developed in his curriculum development and teaching at Think Inc.! Rob Kaplan adds amazing skill with words to bring the message to a professional audience.

Strategic Negotiation adds to the negotiation literature by turning the current state of negotiation training into a process that organizations can institutionalize—a process that helps organizations create measurable business value for themselves and for their customers. As such, it can help you and your organization negotiate more effectively and will earn its place as part of the toolkit for all serious negotiators.

—Max H. Bazerman, Jesse Isador Strauss Professor of Business
 Administration–Harvard Business School, and Vice-Chair of
 Research–Program on Negotiation, Harvard Law School

THE BASICS

1

WHY A PROCESS?

If you've been involved in sales long enough, you may remember a time when selling was considered by most of its practitioners to be more of an art than a science. True salespeople, it was thought, were born, not made. You either "had it," or you didn't. Curiously, despite this widespread belief in a genetic predisposition toward sales success, it was still believed that, because selling was ultimately a matter of people skills, anyone could become a successful salesperson by learning those skills. Training methods emphasizing them were accordingly devised to achieve that end. But all that changed in the early 1980s. Following the publication of a now-classic *Harvard Business Review* article by Thomas V. Bonoma titled "Major Sales: Who Really Does the Buying" (1 May 1982) and the book *Strategic Selling* by Stephen Heiman and Bob Miller, many consultants, salespeople, and individuals in sales management began looking at selling—particularly business-to-business selling—in a different way. They stopped thinking of it as a series of behaviors and started thinking about it as an analytical business process aligning the customer's needs with the seller's capabilities.

They recognized that devising a repeatable, measurable—and therefore improvable—sales process that enabled them to understand customer needs and present business solutions would increase revenues in a way that relying on the human relationship skills of individual salespeople could not. Rather than simply attributing a drop in sales in the previous year to its being a "bad year," for example, having a process would make it possible for them to determine exactly what happened that made it a bad year. It would, in other words, allow them to determine what was causing problems and to do something about it. At the same time, it would enable them to understand their successes and, accordingly, be able to repeat them. In addition, having a process would mean that, rather than simply relying on increasing the number of sales calls to increase sales, they could increase the quality and effectiveness of those calls in a systematic way. Perhaps not surprisingly, as soon as sales and account management people recognized the benefits of such systems, they began to develop both sales processes and training programs to teach those processes to their sales forces. Today, the vast majority of salespeople use those very same processes.

WHAT A STRATEGIC NEGOTIATION PROCESS CAN DO FOR YOU

Despite the creation and implementation of these sales processes, there was still one area of sales that was considered, and is *still* considered, a tactical, reactive, and behavioral art: the art of negotiating. Because of the way business was conducted in the past, the fact that no established processes for sales negotiating existed didn't present any particular problems. However, the same market forces that 20 years ago drove sales to shift from a personal relationship model to a more process-oriented and analytical one are now driving the need for a new approach to negotiating. In fact, the enormous changes that have taken place, both in business in general and in the negotiating environment in particular, have made a Strategic Negotiation Process essential.

To get a better understanding of exactly what those changes are, we recently conducted a survey among salespeople. Although we were, of course, already aware of some of the changes, we discovered, somewhat to our surprise, that they are even more dramatic than we had thought. Among those surveyed:

- 85 percent say negotiations have become increasingly more complex.

- 74 percent report having to face more professional buyers in the marketplace.
- 67 percent say they're seeing increased irrational behavior among their competitors.
- 63 percent report that customer relationships are becoming increasingly long term rather than short term.
- 85 percent say that more internal negotiation is now taking place than in the past.
- 58 percent report seeing major consolidations on both the buyer and seller sides.

But what do all these numbers mean? Exactly how are they impacting sales negotiations, and in what way do they make the development and implementation of sales negotiation strategies so important? Let's look at them one at a time.

Deals Are Becoming Enormously More Complex

Negotiation is no longer just about agreeing on price. Of course, price is still negotiated, but so are licensing agreements, services, coinvestments, legal clauses, risk sharing, intellectual property rights, and others. Introducing these factors into a negotiation makes the old behavioral approach ineffective because it's reactive and focuses on the words and behaviors of the parties. Using a process in such situations enables those involved in both buying and selling to analyze not just surface behaviors—such as a buyer's insistence on receiving more frequent service—but the underlying business "blueprint," or "structure," of the entire deal. That is, it makes it possible for them to consider and diagram all of the various aspects of an agreement rather than fall into the trap of concentrating on any one issue.

More Professional Buyers Are in the Marketplace

Even though salespeople, as well as sales and senior management, still see negotiation primarily in terms of behavioral techniques and tactical responses, buyers are increasingly being trained to see negotiation as a process. This enables them to analyze situations and develop appropriate data to deal with those situations, which in turn provides them with an advantage over the sellers who haven't done such analyses and accordingly have no choice but to simply react to whatever they're presented with. One of the ways buyers take advantage of this is to concentrate on price during negotiations. They do this because they know that salespeople, not having done the same kind of analyses, will be unable to counter their arguments regarding price with compelling arguments for the value of other elements of the deal.

Competitive Behavior Is Becoming Increasingly Irrational

Because of an inability—or unwillingness—to think long term, more and more salespeople are making concessions that are not in the best interests of either themselves or their companies in their efforts to "close the deal." Compounding the problem, their competitors, who are equally unable to see beyond the current quarter, respond by making equally ill-advised concessions. Despite claims that "it's just this one deal," these concessions become the norm. This in turn leads to price wars that, because of the speed at which market data is communicated today, erupt more quickly, go deeper, and are more damaging than were those of the past. Instituting negotiation processes would enable these companies to think about these issues in advance and, if not able to avoid them entirely, be able to develop more effective and proactive responses to them.

Relationships Are Becoming Increasingly Long Term

Such relationships are, of course, beneficial to both sides, but the traditional "one-up" approach to negotiating is not conducive to either developing or maintaining them. When, for example, a salesperson "gets one-up" on a customer, or a customer beats a salesperson so badly that all the profit margin is taken out of a deal, neither side is likely to relish the idea of continuing to do business together. And even if they do continue, the next time both sides will be inclined to do whatever they can to "get even," which, of course, makes an extended relationship even less likely. Using a negotiation process makes it possible to build long-term relationships by using tools other than discounting because, like most classic sales processes, a negotiation process focuses on creating and demonstrating long-term business value for both the customer and the seller.

There's More Internal Negotiation within Companies

Salespeople are increasingly being asked to sell their company's "total value proposition," to bundle the company's solution to its customers. Although this can obviously present substantial benefits to both the company and its customers, negotiating such sales can be extremely difficult for the salespeople involved. Rather than dealing internally with a single product or department manager, they now have to deal with several, each of whom has his or her own P&L (profit and loss), and is, accordingly, more interested in his or her bottom line than in working with the others to do what's best for the company. In addition, because each department tends to have its own ideas of how to negotiate, as well as its own goals, salespeople frequently find that internal negotiations are more difficult than external ones. On the other hand, if a company has a negotiation process in place, the various departments have a common goal as well as a common way of negotiating, which, while not entirely eliminating internal negotiations, can reduce it substantially.

Buyers—and Sellers—Are Merging and Consolidating

As a result of consolidations, there is an increasingly smaller number of players. Because there are fewer players at the same time that the actual number of transactions has gone down, the size—as well as the strategic and financial importance—of those deals has gone up. As a result, buyers and sellers have become more dependent on each other—the seller because a larger percentage of its revenue is tied to one customer, and the buyer because the seller now controls a larger percentage of its supply chain. In other words, buyers and sellers have a different kind of relationship—a more symbiotic one—than they did in the past. Where the traditional approach has both sides negotiating over an ever-shrinking profit margin, a process-oriented approach enables buyers and sellers to address their new relationship by focusing first on creating value for both sides and then determining how to share that value so that both benefit.

But this trend affects buyers and sellers in another way as well. In the past, so many deals were being made that they were of necessity being made entirely independently of each other. Because of that, there was little consistency in either goals or approach on the seller's part. Perhaps even more important, when different tactics were employed by different people in the same organization, buyers—and competitors—perceived the seller's strategy to be something other than what was intended, resulting in a kind of "strategy by default." Using a process by which to conduct negotiations enables companies to establish a common goal, strategy, and tactics. This, in turn, makes it possible for them to more systematically signal their true intent to both customers and competitors and, ultimately, achieve their business objectives.

Finally, not only are there fewer companies in any given industry, those that remain are becoming increasingly dependent on national and global accounts. Salespeople and account managers, who have moved from selling "price and product" to selling "value and solutions," have instituted account management processes that have enabled them to develop consistent—and effective—approaches to these large, complex, and highly profitable customers. However, because no similar processes have been instituted for negotiations, few of these salespeople have been trained to negotiate "value and solutions." Instead, they fall back on the same kinds of tactics they used when selling "price and product." As a result, not only do they give up greater discounts than they should, they also make buyers distrustful of what they'd been told in the first place. Using a process enables them to avoid tactically reactive, price-only, value-dividing discussions and move toward more strategic, multiple-issue, value-creating negotiations.

•   •   •   •   •

Amazingly, despite the fact that, as our survey showed, so many people are aware of the need for a more professional approach to negotiation, corporate America continues to think of negotiation as an "elective" rather than a "required" course in sales training. And despite the numerous benefits of looking at negotiation as an analytical process, most negotiation texts and training still focus on long lists of tactics, countertactics, effective questions, effective responses, personality-type analyses, and the like. As a result, most individuals and organizations are essentially still operating under the "old" rules. In fact, among the sales-people we surveyed:

- 85 percent report that they still use a "reactive" approach to negotiation.
- 85 percent say they have no predetermined strategy for irrational competitor behavior.
- 71 percent report poor internal alignment on negotiation goals or processes.
- 81 percent say they have no formal negotiation process.

Some of the reason for these responses, beyond the lack of updated training, is no doubt simply that people have an apparently natural re-luctance to do anything differently than they have done in the past. As Machiavelli wrote in *The Prince:*

> It must be considered that there is nothing more difficult to carry out, nor more doubtful of success, nor dangerous to han-dle, than to initiate a new order of things. For the reformer has enemies in all those who profit by the old order, and only luke-warm defenders in all those who would profit by the new order, this lukewarmness arising partly from fear of their adversaries . . . and partly from the incredulity of mankind, who do not truly believe in anything new until they have actual experience of it.

My colleagues and I recently had a taste of that kind of incredulity in a recent conversation with an editor at one of the premier sales maga-zines in the world. We were talking with her about the advantages of a repeatable, process-oriented approach to effective business negotiation when she said, "How can you have a consistent process? Aren't negotia-tors like drunks?" When we probed further to find out exactly what she meant by this, she told us that, like a drunk, you can never tell what a ne-gotiator is going to do from one minute to the next, not even in a single negotiation, much less from one negotiation to another. Unfortunately, a great many people share this misconception. And it's because they do, that so much of today's negotiation training still concentrates on developing long lists meant to cover every possible scenario that might ever come up in a negotiation.

But there's also another reason that people continue to use this old style of negotiating. Although the highly tactical and behavioral approach is very difficult to remember, difficult to transfer to others, and inconsistent in terms of success, it does work, at least sometimes. That fact makes this approach to negotiating not unlike gambling—every now and then people win, so they keep going back, even though on average they lose. But as I've suggested, and as I'll prove in this book, giving up that old way of looking at negotiation and embracing our Strategic Negotiation Process will greatly improve the odds of your conducting negotiations that are successful not only from your point of view but also from the point of view of those on the other side of the table.

I'll show you that, although you don't realize it, virtually every negotiation you've ever been, or ever will be, involved in follows a consistent pattern. I'll show you that almost all the tactics that those on the other side of a negotiation throw at you fall into only three categories and that you can prepare for them in advance, whether you have five minutes or five days to prepare. In short, I'll present you with a systematic and rational process that will enable you to establish practical and effective ways of dealing with all of these situations, and go beyond "win-win" to the creation of true, measurable business value.

WHAT A STRATEGIC NEGOTIATION PROCESS CAN'T DO FOR YOU

Of course, I'm realistic enough to know that there are very few—if any—complete solutions to any problem. Despite the many benefits of our Strategic Negotiation Process, there are some problems that even it can't solve. Many negotiation problems, in fact, stem from a poorly executed or nonexistent sales process. Poor account selection is one example. If you sell for a firm that prides itself on providing value and solutions versus the lowest cost, and you choose to call on customers who don't share those values, you are creating problems that, though unrelated to negotiations, will nevertheless have an impact on those negotiations.

Just as account selection can affect negotiation, so too can the negotiation tactics used by your predecessors. Let's say, for example, that you're brand-new in a territory, and you're following a sales rep who, for years, gave away price and service to close deals at the end of each quarter. Unfortunately, even though you may be new, your customers are going to remember, and when negotiation time comes around, they're going to expect the same from you as they got from your predecessor.

The level of the individuals on whom you choose to call can also have an effect on negotiations. If, for example, you're trying to sell fuel to an airline and are calling on the lowest-level purchasing agent selling price per gallon, the chances are you'll end up with negotiation problems. If, on the other hand, you call on executives on multiple levels in the organization, and sell a solution that includes not only fuel but also the benefits of that fuel, such as lowering long-term maintenance costs because of the fuel's high quality, whatever negotiation pressure you encounter will be more easily handled. No doubt you've heard the phrase "You negotiate what you sell," and I couldn't agree more. In fact, it's the combination of effective sales and negotiation processes that will yield the best results for improving your odds in the negotiation marketplace.

But it's not only ineffective or nonexistent sales processes that cause negotiation problems. Other aspects of a deal, although not directly connected to negotiations, can have an impact on them. For example, we've worked with many clients over the years who have products that are priced too high, quality that's too low, or technology that's out-of-date relative to their competitors. Not surprisingly, these firms experience many sales and, subsequently, negotiation problems, which is why they turn to consultants for solutions. But these aren't the kinds of problems that can be fixed with a training class on a negotiation process. These are value-proposition problems, and they can't be negotiated away. Having to compete against a firm that has a better, faster, cheaper alternative to your product or service can only be rectified in the long term by correcting your own company's value proposition.

There is, finally, one other area in which our Strategic Negotiation Process cannot provide the solution to a problem. Because of the nature of the process, it is effective only when there is more than one item to be negotiated, and the more items there are, the more effective it can be. For that reason, if you're selling a service or product that's a commodity, that is, one for which the only variable is price, a negotiation process can provide you with very little benefit. Fortunately, however, there are very few real commodities. In the vast majority of negotiations, even though it may appear at first that price is the only item, if you look further you will almost invariably find that there are other items that can—and should—be part of the negotiation.

WHY THIS BOOK

This is not quite like any other sales negotiation book you've ever read. Although it does, like others, include numerous personal stories and anecdotes, these stories aren't included to show you what a genius I am or how successful I've been as a negotiator. They're included to provide examples of a practical, repeatable, research-based process that you can start to use even before you've finished reading the book. Nor does it include numerous tips and tricks that I've devised over the years that work extremely well—but only if you're me. Rather, it provides a step-by-step approach to a process that's based on the way real people do real business in countries—and cultures—all around the world.

The process works because on a certain level all negotiations are the same, regardless of where they're taking place or who's conducting them. As a result, in broad terms, regardless of whether you're selling tires in Ohio or computer hardware in Nepal, there is a blueprint that can be applied to the negotiation. Of course, the details vary from one deal to another, but that's where the process comes in. It's the process that enables you to fill in those details. In fact, although this book presents the process of filling in the blueprint from a seller's perspective, the blueprint, because of the similarity in all negotiations, can actually be used by those on *either side* of a negotiation, as well as in *any kind* of negotiation. In the next chapter, I show you exactly what that blueprint looks like and begin to show you how, by learning the process, you can become a world-class negotiator.

2

THE STRATEGIC
NEGOTIATION PROCESS

In the last chapter I argued that a blueprint exists that can be applied to literally any negotiation, that by using the Strategic Negotiation Process you can fill in the details of that blueprint, and that by the time you've done that, you'll have all you need to close any deal. The obvious questions then are these: Exactly what is this blueprint, what is the process, and how does the process work? In this chapter I provide the answers to the first two questions, and in the chapters that follow the answer to the third.

THE BLUEPRINT

Our research and global fieldwork have shown that virtually every negotiation, regardless of who's conducting it or where it takes place, can be blueprinted in exactly the same way. This is extremely important, because we also found that everything that takes place in the course of a negotiation—the planning and the research as well as all the tactics used in the final face-to-face meeting—is ultimately driven by that blueprint. But what is it? It's essentially a picture of the entire negotiation, a picture that can be determined by answering two questions for those on both sides of any deal:

1. What are the consequences if we do not reach agreement?
2. What items are likely to be included if we do reach agreement?

To answer these questions, however, we must first go back to some very basic concepts about negotiating. In most negotiations, both sides have a separate "Wish List" of what they would like to achieve in the negotiation. Looking at it graphically, these two Wish Lists could look like this:

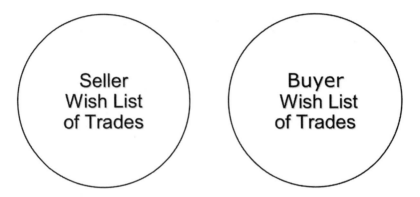

Although neither side in most negotiations gets exactly what it wants in the final deal, if the two sides do come to an agreement, both get at least some of the things that were on their Wish Lists. Such a situation could be represented like this:

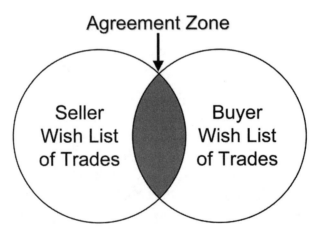

But regardless of whether the two parties ever come to an agreement, there is a blueprint that can be applied to the situation. That blueprint looks like this:

Agreement Zone

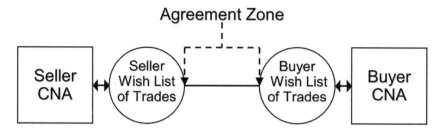

In the middle of the blueprint are the two Wish Lists and between them the Agreement Zone—that is, the place where the two sides meet if they come to an agreement. However, there is always, for both sides, an alternative to reaching agreement with the other side, which we refer to as the Consequences of No Agreement (CNA) and which are shown on either side of the blueprint.

What Are the Consequences of No Agreement?

You may never have used the expression *Consequences of No Agreement,* but the chances are that you've thought about them. After all, you know that *something* is going to happen if you don't make a deal. As the seller, your Consequences of No Agreement—your alternative to making a deal—is most likely going to be losing the sale. Your customer, on the other hand, generally has three possible alternatives to reaching agreement with you. He or she can (1) go to a competitor, (2) build the solution himself or herself, or (3) do nothing. It's only when negotiators obtain something that's at least marginally better than their alternative that they prefer agreement to impasse.

Agreement Zone

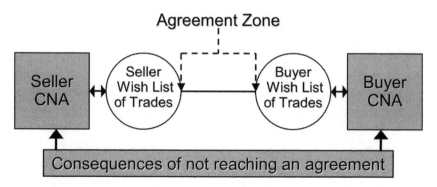

Understanding the Consequences of No Agreement, both for yourself and your customer, is easily the most important aspect of constructing a blueprint of a negotiation. The reason is that, in any negotiation, the other side always sees your offer as a gain or loss based on its perception of the consequences of not reaching agreement with you. Simply put, if the other side believes that making a deal with you will be to its benefit, it will do it. But if it believes that it'll be better off if it doesn't make a deal with you, regardless of the alternatives you're going to lose the sale.

Note that I said the other side makes a decision based on its *perception* of the consequences. The truth is that in any given negotiation, more often than not, one or both sides haven't taken the time to analyze their true Consequences of No Agreement, or they have but have misdiagnosed them. In either case, even if one or the other side is putting a great offer on the table, chances are the two sides won't be able to reach agreement if the consequences are misdiagnosed or misunderstood. That's one of the reasons it's so important to answer the first question I posed above—What are the consequences if we do not reach agreement?—by accurately determining those consequences. Making that determination is the first step in blueprinting a negotiation as well as the first step in the Strategic Negotiation Process. Moreover, as you learn how to use our process in the following chapters, you'll learn how to diplomatically educate those on the other side about their true Consequences of No Agreement. And as you no doubt already understand, most customers will be much more likely to close a deal if they can see that your offer is better than their alternative—that is, their Consequences of No Agreement.

What Items Are Likely to Be Included If We Do Reach Agreement?

Obviously, some negotiations—probably even most—end in agreement rather than impasse. But in order to reach such agreement, in order to fill in the rest of the blueprint, it's necessary to answer the second question I posed: What items are likely to be included if we do reach agreement? In the course of our consulting, we see people involved in very complicated negotiations that include a variety of different items, such as price, length of agreement, service, payment terms, legal terms, volume, and so on. Even so, when we ask them to tell us what the negotiation is about, they often just say, "Price." Bear in mind that these are not young, inexperienced negotiators but rather seasoned executives who may have negotiated hundreds of deals but still fall prey to this common mistake. As I've already noted, except for commodities, of which there are very few, price is never the only item in a negotiation, and unless you know what all the items are going to be, unless you answer the question I raised above, you won't be able to negotiate as successfully as you should.

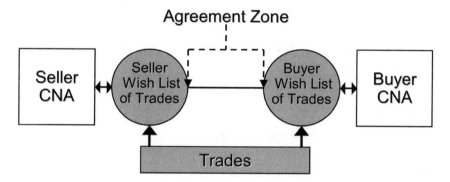

Here's an example. At the end of the first year of my partnership with Max Bazerman, I realized that as a result of the terms of our agreement, Max had received a larger portion of the company's profits than I had. This was not what I'd expected, and although I didn't really need the additional cash, my ego was involved, so I wasn't happy about it. Unfortunately, the only option was to try to renegotiate the deal with him. And that made me more than a bit nervous because Max is, after all, the master. In any case, I called Max and asked him to lunch.

During lunch we discussed a number of items, and it was only when we got near the end of the meal that I brought up the subject of our agreement. "Max," I said, "I'm not making enough money here." Leaning back in his chair, he thought for a moment, looked me in the eye, and said, "So you want some of mine." Although I was, to put it mildly, stunned by his response, I quickly realized what I'd done. I had asked Max to literally reach into his wallet and give me some money back. If he had agreed to do so, I may have made some money, but it would have been at his expense, and, on balance, all we would have accomplished was to "rearrange value." That is, the partnership would have gained nothing by it. And it was essentially because I had, however unwittingly, broken a very important rule of negotiating: Never negotiate one thing. It's only when you discuss more than one thing that you can create true and measurable business value in a negotiation.

When I regained my composure, I said to Max, "No, that's not what I said, although I guess it is what I meant." And Max, to his credit, responded in the masterly way I should have expected of him. He suggested two alternative arrangements between us. In the first, I would get less cash flow than I had been getting at the time, but I would, in turn, get some of his equity. In the second, although I would have additional cash flow, I would give up some of my equity. As it happened, at the time Max was looking for some additional cash himself, and because I was otherwise satisfied with the arrangement, we restructured our deal using the first alternative.

The point here is that rather than negotiate over just one issue—money—we redefined the negotiation in terms of a couple of simple variables that had different levels of importance to the two of us. That is, it was less important to Max that he maintain his share of the partnership's equity as long as he could have greater cash flow. And at the same time, it was less important to me that I have increased cash flow if I could have more equity in the business. In other words, it was the fact that we had something we could trade that made it possible for us to make a deal. In this case, the Consequences of No Agreement would have been either to break up our partnership or to continue it with some bad feelings on both sides. Instead, by trading we both came out of the negotiation better off than we would have if we hadn't reached an agreement.

In theory, determining what items should be part of the final deal should be a very simple exercise. However, because of financial pressures, political pressures, lack of planning, and a lot of old school negotiation tactics, it's not unusual to see situations in which neither side has a clear idea of what it really wants from a negotiation. Of course, both sides always have some idea of what they're looking for—at least one or two items, but often that's all. That's not a problem if you're negotiating over a commodity, but the less commodity-like your product or service is, the more important negotiation skills become and the more opportunity there is for creating value for both sides. The reality is that the heart and soul of business negotiation is *trading*. And to trade properly, a world-class negotiator has to understand not only what all the variables are in a business deal but also what's most to least important to both sides. In the next few chapters, as you learn how to blueprint a negotiation using the Strategic Negotiation Process, you will become that kind of world-class negotiator.

THE STRATEGIC NEGOTIATION PROCESS

At its most basic level, the Strategic Negotiation Process is a step-by-step system that enables you to blueprint a negotiation by making it possible for you to see and understand a negotiation from your own perspective as well as that of your customer. Once you've gained this understanding, our process further enables you to manage the negotiation in such a way as to not only achieve a "win-win" situation but to make it possible for both you and your customer to come away from the negotiation with more than you anticipated going into it. In other words, it enables you to create true, measurable business value and go well beyond the concept of "win-win."

But to understand what the process really is, you're going to have to start thinking differently about what *negotiation* really is. The traditional view of negotiation is, of course, sitting across the table from someone and promising, cajoling, threatening, or using any of a wide variety of tactics to get what you want from that someone. But that meeting is only—or should only be—the final step in a multistep process. Defining *negotiating* as only that face-to-face meeting is like referring to this book simply as *publishing*. In fact, the process that resulted in this book started a long time before you picked it up in a bookstore or ordered it on Amazon. I came up with the idea for it and found a coauthor to work with me; an agent agreed to represent us, and a publisher offered to publish it; we wrote it, and it was designed, printed, bound, jacketed, and so on and so on. In other words, the book you're holding in your hands is only the final step in the process. And it's no different with negotiating. Negotiation doesn't start when you sit down with someone to work out the terms of a deal. It starts as soon as you select an account and start selling. It's *all* negotiation, and redefining it as a process is what leads to world-class deal making.

The Strategic Negotiation Process essentially consists of four steps: (1) Estimating the Blueprint, (2) Validating the Estimation, (3) Using the Blueprint to Create Value, and (4) Using the Blueprint to Divide Value. Before you take the first step, though, it's important for you to establish a goal for any negotiation in which you may be involved. One of the mistakes people often make is trying to plan how to get there before they've even determined where they want to go. Establishing a goal, or not doing so, can have an impact, not only on the planning and execution of a negotiation, but also on any long-term relationship between you and your customer. Interestingly, our research has shown that, more often than not, even when people do have goals in their negotiations, those goals are often inappropriate and, ultimately, counterproductive. In the next chapter I show you how to establish a value-creating goal that is appropriate for any negotiation. In the meantime, following are the four steps of our process.

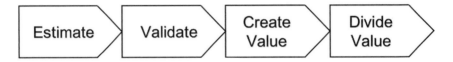

Step One: Estimating the Blueprint

This first step has a twofold purpose and is accomplished through two exercises. The first exercise, the Consequences of No Agreement (CNA) Estimation, enables you to determine what effects—both positive and negative—not reaching an agreement will have on both you and your customer. This will in turn enable you to determine which of you has more power in a negotiation, as well as the place where both sides prefer agreement to impasse. Ultimately, as you'll see, this is also the most effective, fact-based, relationship-enhancing closing skill there is.

In the second exercise, the Wish List Estimation, you develop lists of all the items you and your customer would ideally like to have in the deal and then determine what's most and least important to each of you. These are the items that both of you will, or should be willing to, trade in order to achieve your goals. This is an essential part of the process because both sides place a different value on the items, and trading—giving up something to gain something that's more important to you—is what enables you to create more value to subsequently divide. By creating value, the Strategic Negotiation Process enables both sides in a negotiation to achieve more than just a "win-win" situation.

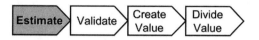

The Consequences of No Agreement and Wish List Estimations together represent a relatively quick step that's based primarily on your own knowledge of the buyer from past deals. They are extremely important, however, because together they form the basis of the blueprint of the deal. And, as I noted before, understanding this blueprint is essential because all the tactical behaviors that both you and your customer use will ultimately be governed by it

Step Two: Validating the Estimation

If Step One represents what you think you know, Step Two is about identifying what you're guessing at or simply don't know about your customer's Consequences of No Agreement and Wish List. That is, it's essentially a fact-finding exercise in which you gather information to determine the accuracy of the estimates you made in Step One. This information is gathered from four different sources: (1) your own knowledge of the customer and your competitors; (2) the knowledge of others in your organization who have worked either for the customer or for your competitor in this deal; (3) publicly available data, such as newspaper articles, annual reports, and the like; and (4) your customer. This last source is, in a sense, the most important because it's in a validation meeting with your customer that you gather the information that enables you to go on to the next step in the process.

Step Three: Using the Blueprint to Create Value

The purpose of the third step in our process is to create measurable business value for those on both sides of a negotiation. In this step, taking into account all the items you've identified in Step One and validated in Step Two, you structure deals in such a way that both you and your customer can get not just what's of primary importance to you but also other benefits that make the deal even more attractive. In other words, by exceeding the Consequences of No Agreement for both sides, you are able to achieve a "win-win" situation. And by trading items, you are able to go beyond "win-win" and increase the value that you and your customer will subsequently divide.

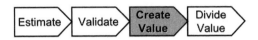

Step Four: Using the Blueprint to Divide Value

In the fourth and final step of the process, you consolidate the data you gathered in the first three steps into a presentation of three or more "Multiple Equal Offers" to your customer. These offers, all of which are equally acceptable to you, provide your customer with more value than he or she had anticipated going into the negotiation, while, at the same time, enabling you to claim as much value as you can without damaging the ongoing relationship. This last step—the face-to-face discussion about terms—is the one that people usually think of when they talk about negotiating. But by the time you've gone through the entire Strategic Negotiation Process and have come to this point, you're in an entirely different situation than the traditional negotiator.

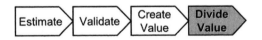

First, because of all the work you've done up to now, you'll find that virtually everything that's said by the customer during this step is either irrelevant to the deal at hand and should be discarded or is related to some aspect of the process and can accordingly be responded to in a reasonable and logical manner. Perhaps even more important, you'll also find when you get to this step, that rather than trying to give as little as you can and get as much as you can from your customer, you'll be in the position of simply dividing a pile of resources that, together, add up to more than either of you ever anticipated.

Some people have suggested that estimating and validating the blueprint just to prepare and present an offer takes too much time and/or won't work in small "pop-up" or ad hoc negotiations. The fact is, though, that neither is true. I've found that taking the time to blueprint negotiations actually saves time for several reasons. First, because of the very nature of using a process, I actually get better and faster each time I do it. Second, it enables me to quickly focus on the most essential data and ignore information that isn't relevant to the negotiation. Third, when others in the organization are familiar with the process, it provides a common language and, as a result, saves a lot of discussion time because everyone is already on the same page. And, finally, because we don't have to spend a lot of time talking about how we're going to conduct the negotiation, we can spend more time discussing what we want out of it and how to get it.

As far as small "pop-up" or ad hoc negotiations are concerned, as you read through this book you'll find many stories about our process being used to blueprint negotiations in just such instances. There is, for example, the story of how someone bought a used boat in a one-hour meeting at a marina, and the one about the salesperson who, when asked for a price reduction for a recently signed contract, was able to respond in 20 minutes. In other words, the process is the same for a $15, 15-minute deal as it is for a $15 million, 15-month deal. Each negotiation is allotted as much time as is available based on the size and importance of the deal. In fact, these are just a few—and not even the most important— benefits of the Strategic Negotiation Process. In the following chapters you will find a great many advantages to learning and using our process to fill in the blueprint. Among the most important of these are that it

- enables you to see a negotiation from both your side and that of your customer;
- allows you to proactively manage the negotiation so that both sides benefit;
- is applicable to virtually any kind of negotiation, regardless of how large or small the deal;
- makes it possible for you to determine what you've done right and repeat it or done wrong and correct it;
- enables you to deal effectively with any kind of negotiating tactic;
- increases the quality of internal negotiation;

- helps you anticipate and deal with irrational competitive behavior and respond in a logical and sensible way;
- fosters long-term relationships with your customers by building real business value;
- allows companies to develop common goals, strategy, and tactics; and
- enables organizations to integrate negotiation more fully into the sales process.

Finally, even though there are clearly benefits to blueprinting negotiations and using the process isn't hard, I must also admit that it does take a little getting used to. But in that respect it's no different from learning to ride a bike or drive a car. If you think back to the first few times you tried to do either of those, you'll remember that it took you a little while before you felt proficient. On the other hand, of course, you're not exactly a neophyte when it comes to negotiating. In fact, whether you realize it or not, at one time or another you've probably done just about all the things that are done in the process. The difference is that you didn't see them as part of a process, and you didn't put them all together. Putting them all together, along with learning and using the process, is what will take you to the level of a world-class negotiator.

You may find, though, certain aspects of the process to be a struggle. All I can tell you is to stick with it. If you do, you'll find that after you've done several business deals this way, it will become your new "intuitive" way of negotiating. After a while, you won't even have to think about the process for blueprinting a deal. In fact, after many years of practice and thousands of live negotiations, I've found that I continue to become more proficient at it, getting better at small pieces of the process each time I use it.

Again, I know there's no one solution to every problem—business is just too complex for that. At the same time, after working through many negotiations using the Strategic Negotiation Process, I've found that they all follow the same pattern. Of course, the details of the Consequences of No Agreement and the items that need to be agreed on change, but the structure remains the same. And because it does, the skills required to diagnose and proactively manage the process remain the same as well. So while blueprinting a deal won't solve all your problems, it *will* change the odds in your favor so that you do well in negotiation more often than not. And the best way to do that is to keep the blueprint—and the process—in mind.

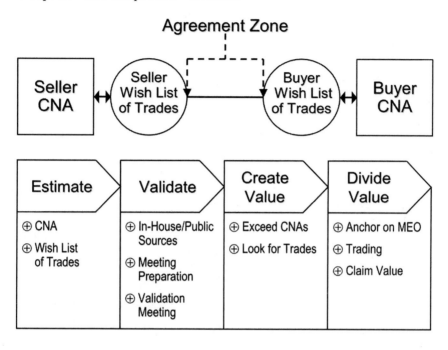

In the remaining chapters I show you how to blueprint a deal using the four-step process. They say that the first step of any journey is always the hardest, and that's true of the journey you're about to take. The first step in the process, Estimating the Blueprint, is the most difficult, but the remaining steps flow logically—and easily—from it. And by the time you're finished you'll find that, in the end, it wasn't all that difficult after all. But even more important, by the time you're finished you'll find that you've become a world-class negotiator.

3

ESTABLISHING A NEGOTIATION GOAL

Before you take the first step in the process of blueprinting a negotiation, it's important to think about why you're conducting the negotiation in the first place, what you hope to get out of it: the goal. This may seem obvious to you, but you'd be surprised how many people enter into negotiations without giving much— if any—thought to why they're doing it. Most of us focus on *what* we are doing, the tactics of the negotiation, rather than on *why*. And as I mentioned before, the goal you set, or the lack of a goal, can have a significant effect, not only on the negotiation and its outcome, but on any long-term relationship you may hope to establish with your customer. So setting a goal is an extremely important part of the process.

SELECTING A NEGOTIATION

The best way to set a goal, in fact the best way to learn how to use our process, altogether, is to start off with a particular negotiation in mind. Think about the deals you're currently involved in or are about to get involved in. By selecting one of them to use as an example and following it through the entire process, you'll not only learn how to blueprint negotiations but you'll be able to start doing it right away. You should bear in mind, though, that to derive the most benefit from learning the process, the situation you select should have certain traits regarding its complexity, its ongoing nature, and its timing.

First, it should be a negotiation that is fairly complex, that is, one in which there are several variables to be negotiated. Negotiations usually involve numerous variables, and it's actually the existence of those variables that makes the process so beneficial. So the more variables in the situation you select, the more benefit you'll be able to realize from the process. It's for this reason that the Strategic Negotiation Process is not applicable to negotiations over commodities—products or services for which price is the only variable. As I've already noted, however, there are very few such products or services. There are normally at least some variables—such as price, volume, or payment terms—in any negotiation.

Second, it should be a negotiation with someone with whom you have, or hope to have, an ongoing relationship. This is because if the deal you select will be a one-time event, you'll have a different perspective on what may occur during the negotiation. Although our process can be applied in virtually any negotiation, it has been designed to be of maximum benefit in situations in which you will be doing at least two deals, you're already in a relationship, or you're hoping to get into a relationship with the customer.

Finally, the situation you choose should be one in which you are not so early in the sales process that there's still a lot of selling to do, but not so late that the deal is very far along. Selling and negotiating are—or should be—intimately connected, but they're not the same thing, and if you're at an early stage in the sales process, you need to continue executing that process before beginning to blueprint the deal. At the same time, one of the greatest benefits of the process is that it enables you to develop a strong negotiation plan well before you start a conversation with a customer. So the earlier you begin the process, the better and more effective your plan will be. In this respect, the best situation to select

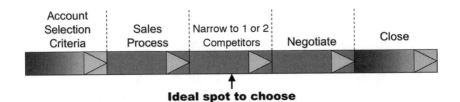

Ideal spot to choose

is one in which the customer has decided that it's either you or someone else, and it's time to start talking "deal terms."

Once you've selected a negotiation to use as an example, think about the goal you'd like to attain for this particular deal, and write it down here. Don't worry about making it perfect—just get it down. Later in the chapter I'll come back to consider this goal again.

COMMON GOALS

One of the things we've learned in our work with negotiators in all types of industries in almost every continent on the globe is that there's a remarkable consistency in negotiation goals. In other words, when I ask people about their goals for any given negotiation, they almost invariably answer with one of a handful of responses. Interestingly, one of the most common of these is "I don't have a goal." For some reason, many people just don't think about what they're trying to accomplish before going into a negotiation. But even among those who do think about it and can provide specific answers to the question, there's a great deal of consistency. Most of the answers I get—regardless of industry or location—are some variation on one of the following:

- "To close the deal by the end of the quarter"
- "To achieve a revenue increase of 12 percent"
- "To maintain or increase our market share"
- "To gain as much information as possible about the other side"

These may all seem like reasonable—even laudable—goals. But when you look more closely, they may not seem quite so laudable as they do at first glance. The real test of the validity—or, perhaps more correctly, the benefits—of these goals is how achieving them will influence the negotiation itself, the results of the negotiation, and any long-term relationship with your customer. Let's see how each of them bears up under that kind of scrutiny.

As already noted, when I ask people about their negotiation goals, a great many of them tell me that they have no goals at all. This is, at least in part, because they approach negotiation with a tactical rather than a strategic mind-set and, as a result, are much more concerned with figuring out how to get there than they are with where to go. This is a problem because, among other things, not knowing where you want to go can make it very difficult—if not impossible—to get there.

More specifically, having no goal can affect the negotiation in several ways. If you don't know what you want to achieve in a negotiation, you can spend a lot of time and effort negotiating hard for items that seem important at the time but aren't really key to making the deal. Perhaps even more important, if you don't have a clear picture of what success means in any given negotiation, you won't be able to recognize a successful deal when you see one. Not having a goal can also have an impact on a long-term relationship with your customer by forcing you to focus on short-term wins that can damage both long-term relationships and profitability.

Even when you do have a goal, however, and regardless of what it may be, if there are multiple people within your organization who are involved in some way in the negotiation, and they're not in agreement about the goal and/or how to attain it, you're going to run into major problems. In fact, making sure everyone in your organization is on the same page is important for several reasons. For one, not being aligned with your internal stakeholders can create an atmosphere of distrust with those you have to rely on to get deals done, which can seriously detract from internal relationships. Moreover, such distrust not only makes internal negotiations more complex on any particular deal, it also makes the next round of internal negotiations more difficult. In other words, the earlier these internal stakeholders are consulted and agree on a common goal and tactics to achieve it, the easier your job is going to be.

As for the specific goals themselves, the first one on the list, "To close the deal by the end of the quarter," isn't really a goal at all—it's a tactic and a dangerous one at that. Our purchasing clients tell us that they know exactly when the quarter and the year end for their salespeople and account managers because that's when they're offered the biggest discounts. This presents negotiation problems for several reasons. First, it can create false time constraints that put unnecessary pressure on the negotiating process. Second, it often costs money, as those time constraints force salespeople to make concessions they wouldn't otherwise make. And, finally, it has a negative impact on long-term relationships because it can make salespeople resort to short-term, high-pressure closing tactics that are inconsistent with their messages and behavior. It can also teach customers to wait for the end of the quarter to start negotiations. None of this, of course, is meant to suggest that the timing of the close is irrelevant. If the timing is important to you—and it may well be—it's something that should be discussed and, depending on how important it is, something you might be willing to trade to attain your goal. The point is, however, that it shouldn't be the goal itself.

This is equally true of the next two common goals on the list—"To achieve a revenue increase of 12 percent" and "To maintain or increase our market share." Like the "goal" of closing by the end of the quarter, these are also tactics that can create a number of different problems in a negotiation. They affect the negotiation itself because, when simply making more money is your primary measurement of success, your customer can sense it and will respond by doing the best he or she can to keep that from happening. Perhaps needless to say, that will, in turn, make attaining your "goal" even less likely. And even if you do get your 12 percent increase or higher margin, because both traditionally come at the expense of the customer, these goals can only serve to have a negative effect on any long-term relationship you'd like to establish.

Again, as with timing, this doesn't mean that increasing your revenue share or margin isn't something to be considered. If it's one of the things you'd like to achieve, you should think about what else you might be willing to trade with the customer that will make the deal more valuable to him or her to attain it. Moreover, in order to not limit your revenue growth, you should think of it as a range—say 12 to 20 percent—depending on the other variables of the deal.

The last of the most common "goals," "To gain as much information as possible about the other side," is also more of a tactic, a means to an end rather than an end in itself. Going into a negotiation with this as a goal will result only in your spending the whole negotiation looking for data that may or may not have an impact on your making a sale. Moreover, even if you're successful in gathering a great deal of information about your customer, you may not make a sale, and you certainly won't have done anything to help establish a long-term relationship between you. In fact, although all the "goals" presented here may be perfectly reasonable as tactics, thinking of them as goals and acting accordingly can have a negative impact on the planning and execution of a negotiation, as well as on the long-term relationship and profitability of both parties.

AN UNCOMMON GOAL

What, then, is a reasonable goal? What kind of goal can result in both parties walking away from the table with even more value than they expected going into the negotiation? Stop for a moment and think about this as a possible goal: *to create joint value and divide it given concerns for fairness in the ongoing relationship.*

If you're like most of our clients, at this point you're likely to say something like, "Get real! My clients don't do business that way!" or "Buyers are not interested in creating value, much less in being fair!" Or as the top salesperson for one of our Japanese clients once said to us: "You don't understand; the Japanese buyer is like God. We don't have any say; he dictates what we do. And all he cares about is price!" So if that's what you're thinking, it's not surprising.

The fact is, though, that we have convinced some of the top selling and purchasing organizations in the world to adopt the goal we've suggested above in their negotiations. And we've been able to do so for one very good reason: it works. When you create joint value and divide it given concerns for fairness in the ongoing relationship, both sides benefit.

Let's say, for example, that you're trying to sell your product to a customer whose main concern is price. The customer can look at this negotiation in essentially two ways. He can say, "My goal is to get the product for less," and accordingly simply demand a lower price. If you, as the salesperson, accede to his demands, he'll be happy because he'll have gotten what he wants, but you'll be less happy because you won't be making as much money as you'd hoped or—perhaps—expected to.

What if, however, the customer considers his goal to be "to create joint value and divide it given concerns for fairness in the ongoing relationship"? If he's thinking along those lines, he may still suggest that you give him a deeper discount than you're offering, but in return he might offer to agree to a longer-term commitment or higher volume, or to provide you with access to other divisions of his company, none of which would actually cost him anything. In a situation like this, you'd be much more likely to offer a better discount because you'd be getting more of his business. In fact, you would both come out of the negotiation with more than you anticipated going into it. And perhaps even more important, you would have established a positive relationship that's likely to bring you even more business in the future.

"It sounds all right in theory," I hear you say, "but does it really work in practice?" The fact is that it does. Although this is a theoretical situation, it's actually based on a real-life one. My colleagues and I were negotiating with a buyer from an international company who was looking to purchase negotiation training for the company's North American division when we ran into a problem. The customer was asking us for a discount of 20 percent from our normal rates, but we didn't want to concede. He pounded us and pounded us on it until, finally, we made him understand that we just couldn't do it. Moreover, because the demand for our services was high (that is, our Consequences of No Agreement was good), there was also no reason why we should concede.

But the customer had something else we were interested in; in addition to the North American operation, the company had a division in Asia. We'd been trying to break into the Asian market for some time and wanted access to the customer's operation there. But the customer considered us too risky because we hadn't had any experience in that part of the world. So aiming to "create joint value and divide it given concerns for fairness in the ongoing relationship," we made a counteroffer. If, we said, the customer would agree to broaden the consulting contract to include its Asian division as well as the North American one, we would give them the 20 percent discount they were asking for in North America plus another 5 percent when we worked in Asia. We did, however, make it clear that the additional 5 percent in Asia was available only for the first year, and that once we'd proved that our process worked, we would return to our normal pricing. Thus, the customer would pay less than it expected to for our services, and we would get more of its business.

Perhaps not surprisingly, they agreed. In fact, having seen the process in action and realizing how well it worked, the customer subsequently began using our process in negotiations with all its suppliers. The deal was enormously advantageous from our perspective as well. We got our foot in the door in Asia, which led to other Asian customers and, ultimately, higher revenue streams. In fact, because of those new revenue streams, the benefit of this trade far outweighed the cost of providing it.

Thus, aiming to "create joint value and divide it given concerns for fairness in the ongoing relationship" changes the very nature of the negotiation in a variety of positive ways. One of these is helping you create and negotiate larger, rather than smaller, deals because it leads to tactics that are more likely to yield larger deals. As a result, even if it doesn't work every time, in the end you make more money because the individual deals themselves are larger. Another benefit is the positive effect on the atmosphere and tone of the negotiation as a result of sharing the goal with your customers. Of course, those on the other side of the table, not surprisingly, tend to be very skeptical at first. But once you've proved that you mean what you're offering over the course of several negotiations, your sincerity not only makes individual negotiations easier and more productive, it has a positive impact on the ongoing relationship between you and your customer.

I saw very clearly how this works some time ago with one of my tenants. I own, and live in, a building that has several rental apartments. This particular tenant was an actor and, like most young and struggling actors, was always looking for ways to feed himself while he pursued his acting career. One of those ways was a part-time job power washing and sealing patio decks. Every time he had a job to do, though, he had to rent a power washer from Home Depot for about $70 a day. As it happened, I had always wanted a power washer for several home improvement projects but couldn't justify the $400 purchase. So I made a deal with the tenant: I would buy a power washer and rent it to him each time he used it for $35, half of what he was paying. Moreover, he could store it at his house so he wouldn't have to go to Home Depot, wait in lines, or fill out forms, thus saving himself both time and effort. The deal would, however, also be good for me in that his rental payments would be paying off the cost of the power washer. Eventually, I would own it and, even better, have gotten it for free. The deal would actually create $35 of value for each of us every time he used the power washer.

But when I suggested my idea to him, he looked at me suspiciously and said, "How did you come up with a deal like that?" Even though it would clearly benefit both of us, he didn't trust the deal because we've all been conditioned to believe that negotiation is about determining who gets what rather than creating joint value. Despite my tenant's wariness, he agreed to go ahead with it. Not surprisingly, he soon realized exactly how much the deal was benefiting both of us and was delighted with it. Perhaps even more important, because we were both happy with the deal, it helped us establish a relationship that enabled us to subsequently make several similar deals.

THE "MYTH OF THE FIXED PIE"

Ultimately, what we're really talking about here is counteracting what my partner, Max Bazerman, refers to as the Myth of the Fixed Pie. Having spent a great deal of time studying how people negotiate, Max recognized that achieving a "win-win" situation essentially means both sides getting an acceptable share of a fixed "pie" of resources. Of course, a "win-win" solution isn't in itself a bad thing. But if you stop there, even though both sides may have achieved something marginally better than their alternatives, you may still be leaving serious money on the table. Nevertheless, many people do stop there. What Max realized is that the pie isn't necessarily fixed. In almost any negotiation on almost anything other than a true commodity, you can find a way to enlarge the pie—create true, measurable business value and then trade to determine who gets how much of that value.

In terms of the blueprint I showed you in the last chapter, enlarging the pie essentially means increasing the size of the Agreement Zone. Let's say, for argument's sake, that you're involved in a negotiation in which there's $50,000 worth of value in the Agreement Zone. The blueprint for that would look like this:

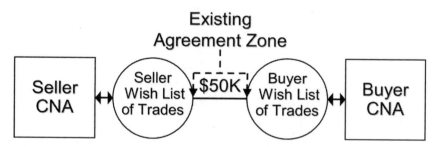

Let's say further, though, that by aiming to "create joint value and divide it given concerns for fairness in the ongoing relationship," that is, by trading a wide range of items in the negotiation rather than just one or two, you can increase the size of the pie, the Agreement Zone, by an additional $50,000 in value. In that case, the blueprint would look like this:

Agreement Zone Made Larger

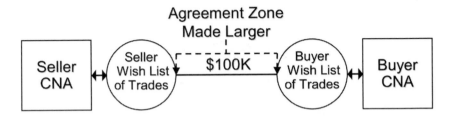

Finally, having enlarged the Agreement Zone, that is, having created more value, you can then divide it, in which case the blueprint might look like this:

Agreement Zone Division

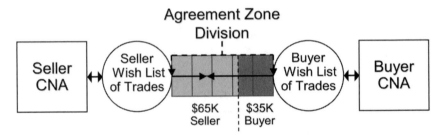

I understand, of course, that making the pie bigger and then determining who gets what share is completely counterintuitive to most people. It's not the way people have traditionally done negotiations. But, as I explained earlier, the traditional way of negotiating simply doesn't work in today's business environment, and a new way is needed. The Strategic Negotiation Process is just such a way.

· · · · ·

Before we go on to the first step of the process, let's go back for a moment and look at the goal you set in the beginning of this chapter for your sample negotiation. Is your goal the same as one of those that most people use? Does it really look like a goal to you now, or does it look more like a tactic—a means to an end rather than an end in itself? It's certainly true that getting the deal done in a reasonable time, increasing revenue or market share, and gaining data on the other side are laud-

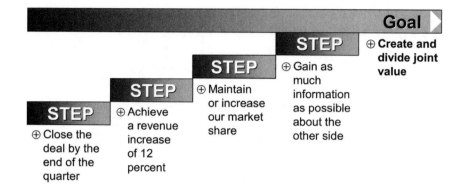

able ambitions and prerequisites to creating joint business value. They do not, however, create joint business value themselves.

Now think again about what you really want to achieve in your sample negotiation, and circle the goal below that now looks most appropriate:

1. Close the deal profitably.
2. Close the deal by the end of the quarter.
3. Create joint value and divide it given concerns for fairness in the ongoing relationship.

I hope you chose Number Three. Bear in mind, though, that choosing Number Three as a goal doesn't mean that you can't close the deal profitably or by the end of the quarter. One of the benefits of using the Strategic Negotiation Process is that if, for example, increasing your revenues is what you want out of a given negotiation, you're much more likely to get it by trading it for something that your customer considers more important.

DEALING WITH *Professional* **B**uyers

I noted earlier that one of the major changes taking place in the negotiating environment is the increasing number of professional buyers in the marketplace. This new type of buyer not only sees negotiation, like sales, as a process but, perhaps even more important for our purposes, is capable of performing in-depth analyses of your solution versus your competitor's to an extent that you probably haven't even begun to imagine. What this means is that many buyers are using what is effectively a new purchasing model, one that enables them to quantify value to a much greater extent than the vast majority of salespeople. Learning how to blueprint negotiations using the Strategic Negotiation Process will go a long way toward helping you meet this challenge. But because this is such a relatively new phenomenon, I am also providing additional information on this specific aspect of negotiating in boxes like this throughout the book.

• • • • •

It may seem unlikely that professional buyers would be interested in being able to "create joint value and divide it given concerns for fairness in the ongoing relationship." The fact is, though, they are, and for one very good reason. They know that in the vast majority of business-to-business deals, the long-term health of both buyer and seller comes not from negotiating over shrinking margins but, rather, from building long-term, profitable business relationships. So even though professional buyers can certainly be very tough negotiators, they understand that both you and they will be better off if you can come to an agreement in which both sides are satisfied.

Best **P**ractices **R**eview

- Always set a goal to "create joint value and divide it given concerns for fairness in the ongoing relationship."
- Communicate that goal to your customer and prove that you mean it through your tactics.
- Remember that setting that goal is about negotiating in a customer-friendly way, but larger deals and more money are the driving force behind it.

Common Mistakes to Avoid

- Confusing tactics for goals. Many tactics, such as achieving a 10 percent price increase, are actually Wish List items that can be traded to achieve your goal of creating and dividing joint value.
- Being fooled by those who say that value can't be created in your industry—except in the case of commodities, value can be created in virtually any negotiation.

• • • • •

Up to this point I've been talking about *what* you want to achieve from a negotiation. Starting with the next chapter—"Step One: Estimating the Blueprint, The Consequences of No Agreement Estimation"— I'll be focusing on *how* you can attain that goal and *how,* by learning to use the Strategic Negotiation Process to blueprint any negotiation, you can become a world-class negotiator.

THE PROCESS

4

STEP ONE
ESTIMATING THE BLUEPRINT

PART ONE

*The Consequences of No Agreement
Estimation*

Now that you've established your negotiation goal—to create joint value and divide it given concerns for fairness in the ongoing relationship—you have to begin the process of making that goal a reality. As already noted, the Strategic Negotiation Process is essentially composed of four steps:

Estimate	Validate	Create Value	Divide Value
⊕ **CNA**	⊕ In-House/Public Sources	⊕ Exceed CNAs	⊕ Anchor on MEO
⊕ Wish List of Trades	⊕ Meeting Preparation	⊕ Look for Trades	⊕ Trading
	⊕ Validation Meeting		⊕ Claim Value

In the first step of the process you begin to blueprint the business deal. Understanding this blueprint is essential because it governs everything that happens in a negotiation, including the tactical behaviors used during the face-to-face aspect of the negotiation. This first step consists of two parts—the Consequences of No Agreement (CNA) Estimation and the Wish List Estimation. These two estimations essentially enable you to answer the two questions: "What are the consequences if we do not reach agreement?" and "What items are likely to be included if we do reach agreement?" In this chapter I focus on using the CNA Estimation to answer the first question.

The purpose of this estimation, as its name implies, is to enable you to determine what effects—positive and negative—not reaching an agreement will have on both you and your customer. "But," you say, "I already know what happens if I don't make the deal. I lose the business." And that may be true. When you're on the selling side, losing the business is the usual Consequence of No Agreement. But every negotiation situation is unique, and what "lose the business" means in this negotiation at this time may be different from what it means in another negotiation at another time. And the only way to know exactly what it means in any given situation is to do this kind of estimation.

Similarly, you may say, "But I know what happens to my customer if he or she doesn't buy from me—the customer goes to one of my competitors." And that may also be true. And then again, maybe not. The fact is that it's even more difficult—and more important—to estimate the other side's Consequences of No Agreement than it is your own. This is because when you get to the point of making an offer, your customer will see that offer as a gain or loss based on how it perceives what happens to it if it doesn't reach agreement with you, that is, the customer's own Consequences of No Agreement.

The chances are, though, that the customer won't have collected realistic facts about its alternative to reaching agreement with you. It'll believe some spiel given to it by your competitors or have convinced itself that it can get whatever it is it needs better, faster, and cheaper elsewhere, even though that may not be true. As the character George Costanza from TV's *Seinfeld* said, "It's not a lie if you believe it." So even though you may be putting a very good offer on the table, the other side may still think it can do better somewhere else. But if you've analyzed its Consequences of No Agreement as well as your own, and you know what will happen to the customer if you don't make the deal, you'll be in a position to diplomatically educate the customer about it and show the customer how accepting your offer is in its best interests.

But simply stating the Consequences of No Agreement for both sides is just the beginning of the process of blueprinting a negotiation.

As you're about to see, once you've determined those consequences, you have to determine their effects, how those consequences will have an impact—both positively and negatively—on both sides, and the extent to which they will make any potential deal attractive or not attractive to both sides.

Estimating both your own and your customer's Consequences of No Agreement will, in turn, enable you to determine who has the true power in a negotiation and the place where both sides prefer agreement to impasse. Determining who has the power is important because it affects how both sides think of the negotiation and, in turn, how they behave. Those who believe they have more power tend to overestimate the value of their offer and, accordingly, behave in a manner that makes impasse more likely and value-creating trades less likely. On the other hand, those who believe they have less power tend to underestimate the value of their offer and "roll over" too quickly, giving up value to the other side. Misdiagnosing who has the power, then, can be detrimental to both you and your customer.

The other key benefit of understanding the Consequences of No Agreement for both sides is that it allows you to determine the place at which both sides prefer agreement to impasse, or what I call the Agreement Zone. This zone is established by figuring out the parameters of the agreement, that is, the least that will be acceptable to both you and your customer. Later in this chapter I show you exactly how to determine the location of the Agreement Zone, and later in the book how to use it as a starting point for building value in your negotiation.

Once you've used the Consequences of No Agreement Estimation to determine who has the power in this negotiation and the location of the Agreement Zone, you'll go on, in the next chapter, to the second part of this step—the Wish List Estimation. This analysis allows you to determine the items that you and your customer would ideally like to have included in the deal if you come to an agreement, including what is most and least important to both of you. These are, again, the items that both of you will trade, or should be willing to trade, to achieve your goal to "create joint value and divide it given concerns for fairness in the ongoing relationship." This is an essential part of the process because you and your customer place different values on these items, and trading—giving up something in order to gain something else of greater value—is what enables you to create more value to subsequently divide.

By "enlarging the pie," the process of blueprinting the negotiation enables both of you to achieve much more than just a "win-win" situation.

Before you begin the Consequences of No Agreement Estimation, however, I'd like you to do one thing. Think about the negotiation example you've selected and ask yourself who has the power in that situation. Is it you or the other side? You'll probably say it's the other side, but you could very well be wrong. One of the things my colleagues and I have learned in our consulting practice with almost 10,000 buyers and sellers over the years is that both almost invariably believe it's the other side that has more power in the negotiation. Of course, sometimes that's true. Even so, virtually all salespeople typically have more power than they think they do, and virtually all buyers typically have less, so both tend to misdiagnose the situation. After you've conducted the Consequences of No Agreement Estimation for your situation, we will revisit this question to decide exactly who does have the power.

THE CONSEQUENCES OF NO AGREEMENT ESTIMATION

The purpose of the Consequences of No Agreement Estimation is to enable you to determine who has the power in the negotiation and the location of the Agreement Zone, the place where both sides prefer agreement to impasse. Doing this essentially requires you to answer three questions for both sides in the negotiation:

1. What are the possible Consequences of No Agreement and which is the most likely?
2. What are the elements of those Consequences of No Agreement that need to be considered?
3. Are those elements hard or soft costs or benefits in the short term and in the long term?

What are the possible Consequences of No Agreement and which is the most likely? As the seller, of course, your most likely Consequence of No Agreement is to lose the sale. The buyer, on the other hand, generally has three possible Consequences of No Agreement:

going to one of your competitors, building the solution itself, or doing nothing. There are, of course, other possible alternatives, but analyzing every one of them is neither feasible nor necessary. In fact, ultimately, at the most basic level, every possible Consequence of No Agreement falls into one of these alternatives. Your decision about which is most likely will be based on your knowledge of the industry, the customer, and the competition.

What are the elements of those Consequences of No Agreement that need to be considered? The elements of each Consequence of No Agreement are those things that will be affected if you don't make a deal and that you and your customer should accordingly take into consideration. Of course, because the same Consequence of No Agreement will have a different effect on the buyer than on the seller, the elements you consider will depend on which side of the table you're on. Let's say, for example, that, as the seller, your Consequence of No Agreement is to lose the sale. In that case, the elements of that Consequence of No Agreement—the things it will affect and that you should consider— would include the following:

- How much revenue this customer represents
- How losing the sale will have an impact on your bonus
- How easy/difficult it will be to replace the customer
- If any internal political ramifications result if you lose this business

Let's say, on the other hand, that you are estimating your customer's Consequences of No Agreement and have determined that the most likely one is for her to choose another supplier. What you need to do, then, is think about how making that decision will affect her—that is, what elements should she be taking into account in comparing you with your competitor. Assuming you are the incumbent, the elements she should be considering would include these:

- How much it will cost the customer to switch from you to your competitor
- How the competitor's product quality compares with yours
- How the competitor's service quality compares with yours

Are those elements hard or soft costs or benefits in the short term and in the long term? Once you've determined the Consequences of No Agreement and the elements associated with those consequences, the next step is to determine whether those elements are minuses or pluses (costs or benefits) and whether they are hard or soft costs or benefits. Hard costs or benefits include anything that's quantitative or measurable— that is, something that can be given a dollar amount, such as increased revenues, training costs, percentages, time, output, or the development of a new product pipeline. Soft costs and benefits, on the other hand, are qualitative and include those things to which it is difficult to attach a metric. These might include political ramifications, risk for the seller, customer satisfaction, ease of use of the product or service by the buyer, or ease of working with the buyer for the seller.

As you can see, many types of elements—whether they are ultimately minuses or pluses—cross industry lines. Things like customer satisfaction, for example, are elements of a customer's Consequences of No Agreement in almost every negotiation, regardless of the business. However, what constitutes short term and long term, and the significance of the difference between them, can vary considerably from one industry to another. For example, one of our clients is a major steel producer that makes, among other things, steel pillars for building construction. During negotiations over a deal with one of its customers, a construction company, the customer told our client it was thinking of using concrete instead of steel for its pillars, as concrete was less expensive. In other words, the customer's Consequence of No Agreement was concrete, and the only element being considered was price.

Our client had to admit that in the short term at their then-current prices, concrete did cost less than steel. Because we had conducted a Consequences of No Agreement Estimation for our client, however, the client was also able to point out that even though the lower price of concrete was a short-term benefit, the "total cost of ownership" in the long term would actually be less for steel because concrete may cost more to maintain and may not last as long as steel. This is just one example of how the difference between short term and long term can have an impact on a specific industry. No doubt you can think of others that are specific to your own business.

Your Side's Consequences of No Agreement

You begin with your own Consequences of No Agreement—the seller's—because it's the simplest. As already noted, the most common Consequence of No Agreement for the seller is to lose the business. But because every negotiation is unique, the effects of that Consequence of No Agreement, that is, the real meaning of "lose the business," changes from one negotiation to another. For that reason, unless you do an estimation of your own Consequences of No Agreement as well as that of your customer, there's no way you can tell exactly what impact it will have on where the power lies or on the location of the Agreement Zone.

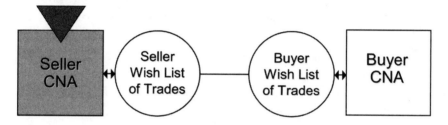

Let's say, for example, that you're in the middle of negotiations over a deal, and your customer is being so tough that you're not sure you'll be able to come to an agreement. At the moment, though, the economy is exploding, you've been Salesperson of the Year for the past three years, you're at 176 percent of your annual goal, and it's only the third quarter. Obviously, although you would of course prefer to not lose the sale, it would hardly mean the end of the world. But what if the economy were in recession, you were only at 65 percent of your sales goal, it was coming down to the end of the fourth quarter, and your job was on the line? Clearly, then, losing the sale would mean something else entirely. The point is that unless you do the Consequences of No Agreement Estimation, you have no way of knowing what your true costs and benefits might be. If you're still not convinced, though, the following story might change your mind.

My partner, Max Bazerman, tells a story beginning with his phone ringing one Sunday night. It's one of his distant cousins, who is in the market for a house. The cousin and his wife have been out looking at houses all day, and they've found one they think is perfect. After providing Max with an excruciatingly lengthy and detailed description of the house, the cousin finally gets to the point. "They've got it listed at $185,000," he tells Max. "We offered $165,000, and they countered with $179,000. What should we do?" Being the expert in negotiation that he is, Max asks, "What will happen if you don't buy the house?" For a moment there is silence on the other end of the phone. And then his cousin replies, somewhat frustrated, "I didn't call you for advice on how *not* to buy a house."

So Max asks the same question again. This time the cousin says, "You don't understand. The next best house has an avocado green 1970's kitchen and it's the same price." But questioning the cousin further, Max discovers that other than the green kitchen, the second house is just as "perfect" as the one they've fallen in love with. Max asks his cousin if it might be possible to get that house for $20,000 less, which would provide them with enough money to remodel the kitchen. The cousin thinks this is a good possibility and decides to go back to the second house's owners to discuss it. Max gratefully goes back to what he was doing when the phone rang.

Max's cousin had gone into the negotiation without having thoroughly analyzed his own Consequences of No Agreement and was convinced that the consequences of not buying the first house were horrible. In fact, Max's cousin did the same thing that most of us do—focus on our own consequences and assume they're much worse than they actually are. On that basis, he also concluded that he had no power in the negotiation. But when Max helped him do the analysis, he recognized that the consequences were not necessarily as bad as he'd anticipated. In other words, Max's cousin was able to change his Consequences of No Agreement for the better and in the process substantially increase his power. Of course, Max's cousin was the buyer in this situation, and we are more concerned here with your Consequences of No Agreement as a seller. But the principle applies regardless of which side of the table you're on.

We recently saw a similar dynamic at work during a client meeting with the major account executive of a U.S-based semiconductor industry supplier. This company was one of the largest in the industry, selling tools and software priced in the $50 million to $300 million range. One of our new consultants, Sam Tepper, a very bright Ph.D. from Northwestern University, was taking the lead in the meeting and asking Consequences of No Agreement–related questions. The account executive just kept shaking her head. "You don't understand," she said. "Our closest competitor is larger, has a more complete solution, and has tools that are more accurate and more reliable. Plus, they're often willing to give those tools away as part of a large deal." What she was telling us was that the buyer had a great Consequence of No Agreement—numerous benefits and virtually no costs—while their own Consequence of No Agreement was to lose the business—which had no benefits and lots of costs.

I had no idea how we might respond to this comment; it seemed like an impossible situation. Sam, however, knew exactly what to say. "My gosh," he exclaimed, "how are you still in business?" The executive seemed stunned by the question. At last, though, she admitted, albeit rather sheepishly, that the company had grown more than 40 percent over the previous year. And, in fact, after we did a Consequences of No Agreement Estimation with them, we found that not only was our client's Consequences of No Agreement better than they thought, but also that their customer's Consequence of No Agreement—choosing a competitor—would actually present them with several costs. We've seen time and time again how sellers can overestimate the impact or effect of their Consequences of No Agreement and underestimate the costs to the other side. That's why it's so important to do the analysis.

Estimating your side's costs and benefits. Having decided that, as the seller, your most likely Consequence of No Agreement is to lose the business, the next step is to determine the elements of that Consequence of No Agreement, that is, the effects it will have, and decide if those elements are hard or soft costs or benefits for the short term and long term. For you as the seller, these elements are essentially those that will have an impact on you, your company, and/or your industry. These might include, for example, sales revenues, sales profits, and your personal financial stake (e.g., a bonus), all of which are hard costs or benefits. They might also include company-related political ramifications, such as your boss's friendship with the customer's executive vice president; industry-related political ramifications, like the message it sends to the market if you win or lose a big customer; and long-term customer relations, all of which are soft costs or benefits. Here's an example of some of the kinds of costs and benefits that might result when a seller loses a sale:

The Seller's Consequence of No Agreement: Losing the Sale

Elements to Be Considered	Cost/Benefit
$100,000 in revenue; costs of sale; my bonus	*Hard Cost*
My boss will not be happy; competitors will get my customer	*Soft Cost*
Market price is 4 percent higher than the client is willing to pay	*Hard Benefit*
The client's toughness on our operations team	*Soft Benefit*

Gathering and recording data. Now it's time for you to determine the elements of your own Consequence of No Agreement—losing the business—as well as determining whether the elements are costs or benefits in your own negotiation. As you begin to gather data on these costs and benefits, you should bear in mind several things.

The first is *the importance of being objective*. You don't have to like what you say here, but it should be as true, or at least as close to the truth, as you can make it. If at this point you knowingly estimate your own Consequences of No Agreement to be greater—or less—than they are, you will be constructing a picture of the situation that's unrealistic and, ultimately, of little use. The first step in becoming a world-class negotiator is arming yourself with facts, not assumptions, and only by being brutally honest will you be able to do that.

Second, in gathering data it's very important for you to *concentrate on the specifics* of this negotiation. Consequences of No Agreement are not something that exists at the market level; they're specific to the particular deal. For that reason, it's essential that in conducting the analysis you bear in mind what customer this is; which competitor or competitors may be involved; what product or service you're offering; the time of year; your current financial condition; whether you are the incumbent; the current market, pricing, and demand for your product or service; and any emerging competitors. Only by concentrating on this specific negotiation will you be able to construct an accurate picture of the situation.

Finally, although as a seller it's not difficult to determine what costs there might be in losing a sale, it's much more difficult to determine what benefits there might be. Our experience suggests that basically only two kinds of benefits are possible to the seller in such a situation, both of which are included in the table above. The first is that if this particular customer has been pushing you hard on price, the chances are you'll be able to replace him or her with a higher-margin customer. The second is that if this is a "high-maintenance" customer—one who has required a lot of time and effort for you to deal with—you may well be better off without him or her.

To help you remember the hard and soft costs and benefits in the short term and long term, we've found it helpful to record them in the format on page 54. As you'll see, we've provided space for six types of data. The first concerns your Consequences of No Agreement. Again, this is supposed to be a simple, straightforward answer to the question "What will happen to us if we don't make the deal?" As I've already noted, the answer to this question is most likely to be "Lose the sale" when you're the seller.

The second, third, fourth, and fifth areas are, respectively, where you record the short-term and long-term hard costs, soft costs, hard benefits, and soft benefits associated with that Consequence of No Agreement. If you have any questions about the differences between these costs and benefits, you can turn back to the section in this chapter in which I discussed them.

The sixth and final section may be the most important one of all. It's there that you record whatever additional information you feel you still need about your costs and benefits. You don't have to concern yourself at this point with where you will get that information; you'll learn that during a later step in the process. For the moment all you have to do is list the data that is needed. (Note, incidentally, that you will find a copy of this—as well as all of the book's other forms—in the Appendix.)

The Other Side's Consequences of No Agreement

Now that you've determined your own Consequence of No Agreement along with the costs and benefits associated with it, it's time for you to estimate your customer's. We very often hear people say that it's difficult, if not impossible, to know the consequences for the other side. And given the fact that most people don't think much about what it might mean to their customer to lose the deal, it's not particularly surprising that they should feel that way. The fact is, though, that, as already noted, your customer really has only three likely Consequences of No Agreement: (1) go to a competitor, (2) build the solution themselves, or (3) do nothing.

CONSEQUENCES OF NO AGREEMENT—OUR SIDE

1. Our Consequence of No Agreement is: _____
_____

2. The short-term and long-term hard costs associated with that Consequence of No Agreement are: _____
_____
_____
_____
_____

3. The short-term and long-term soft costs associated with that Consequence of No Agreement are: _____
_____
_____
_____
_____

4. The short-term and long-term hard benefits associated with that Consequence of No Agreement are: _____
_____
_____
_____
_____

5. The short-term and long-term soft benefits associated with that Consequence of No Agreement are: _____
_____
_____
_____
_____

6. The data we still need about the above is: _____
_____
_____
_____
_____

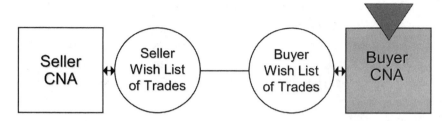

Going to a competitor is the most frequent Consequence of No Agreement for a buyer. This is because, as you know, buyers are almost always convinced that they can get it better, faster, cheaper elsewhere, regardless of what it is, and whether or not it's true. But, as you also know, it's never that simple except in the case of true commodities, of which there are very few. There are always other variables that should be taken into consideration. Doing so, that is, using what you've learned about their needs during the sales and negotiation processes to determine the true costs and benefits of going to one of your competitors versus buying from you, you'll be able to show them why it's in their best interests to buy from you based on *all* the relevant factors, not just price.

Building a solution themselves is probably the next most frequent buyers' Consequence of No Agreement. It's quite common for a customer to believe that its in-house people can build the same solution as yours, custom-made and for less. Sometimes, in fact, it's true. If it is, though, there's something fundamentally wrong with your value proposition. Even though buyers believe they can do it better themselves, more often they can't. And the best way of making them understand that is to compare the actual costs and benefits of their doing it themselves versus hiring you to do it.

Despite what I've called it, doing nothing, the third most likely Consequence of No Agreement, isn't really doing nothing at all. In fact, what it really means is the buyer's taking the resources he or she would have expended on your offer and using them elsewhere. Let's say, for example, that you have a customer who has earmarked $100,000 for a consulting project. You present them with a $100,000 consulting solution, but they come back and say that they've decided not to do anything at this time. Although it may be true that the customer isn't doing anything "externally" with those budget dollars, it may be putting them toward an entirely different project, such as hiring a new salesperson, which is, then, the customer's Consequence of No Agreement. Under those circumstances, your challenge is to compare the costs and benefits of their hiring a new salesperson versus your consulting solution.

Although these three different Consequences of No Agreement may have different costs and benefits associated with them, it's important to bear in mind that regardless of which Consequence of No Agreement is most applicable in any particular situation, it is essentially always a matter of you versus some form of competition. That competition may be another company, the customer doing it himself or herself, or the customer using the budget allocated for your product or service for some other purpose. Remember, too, that your customer will make a decision based on a perception—probably inaccurate—of whether what you have to offer will be a benefit to him or her. For that reason, the best way to prepare yourself for any of these situations is to determine as many costs and benefits associated with both sides' Consequences of No Agreement as you can.

Finally, you may find yourself in a situation in which more than one of these three possible Consequences of No Agreement seems to be appropriate. In that case, for the purposes of the Consequences of No Agreement Estimation, you should select the one that you think is most likely to occur, regardless of which one it might be.

Estimating the other side's costs and benefits. Having decided which of the three possible Consequences of No Agreement is most likely for the other side, the next step is to determine the elements of that consequence and estimate whether they are hard or soft costs or benefits for the short term and long term. For the buyer, the most important of those elements are (1) the prework or design stage, (2) the installation phase, (3) ongoing operations and management, and (4) output, that is, the extent to which the product or service fulfills the business purposes for which the buyer purchased it.

Examples of costs and benefits in the prework or design stage might be ease or difficulty of customization, expense of customization, or the amount of knowledge or experience possessed by the people who are designing the product or service. Costs and benefits in the installation phase might include the ease or difficulty of integrating the product or service into an existing system, training costs, and switching costs (i.e., any expenditure the buyer might have to make as a result of purchasing from a new rather than an incumbent supplier). Among the costs and benefits in ongoing operations and management are ease of use, reliability, and service. Finally, for costs and benefits in the output stage, you might consider whether the product or service results in greater sales, reduced cycle time, fewer errors, or increased capacity. If you consider all these elements, it quickly becomes clear that when a buyer says "It's cheaper elsewhere," all he's done is an incomplete and oversimplified analysis of his Consequences of No Agreement.

Here is an example of the costs and benefits that might result from the most frequent buyers' Consequence of No Agreement: going to a competitor. Remember, this is supposed to be from your customer's perspective, so to do this appropriately you have to put yourself in the customer's shoes. Note here that incumbency plays a large part in the Consequences of No Agreement Estimation, and for this example I'm assuming that you are the incumbent.

The Buyer's Consequence of No Agreement: Going to a Competitor	
Elements to Be Considered	Cost/Benefit
Higher long-term maintenance; higher switching costs; lower output	*Hard Cost*
Hassle of retraining staff	*Soft Cost*
Competitor's price is 9 percent lower in the short term	*Hard Benefit*
Will be a more important client to my competitor than he or she is to me	*Soft Benefit*

Gathering and recording data. Now that you have an idea of how to determine a typical buyer's Consequence of No Agreement and its effects, it's time for you to determine the Consequence of No Agreement for the buyer in your own negotiation. As you gather data on your customer's Consequence of No Agreement and the costs and benefits associated with it, there are several things you should bear in mind.

First, just as it was important to be objective in estimating your own Consequence of No Agreement and its costs and benefits, it's extremely important that you do so in estimating your customer's. As I mentioned earlier, it's not at all unusual for sellers to overestimate the negative effect of their own Consequence of No Agreement and underestimate that of the people on the other side. But if you do that, you're going to create an unrealistic picture of the situation that won't do either you or your customer any good. That's why it's important that you be as honest and objective as you can.

Second, as was also the case with estimating your own Consequence of No Agreement, it's essential in this step that you concentrate on the specifics of this negotiation. Every negotiation is different, so in estimating the Consequences of No Agreement and the costs and benefits of any particular negotiation, it's important that you bear in mind what customer this is; which competitor or competitors may be involved; what product or service you're offering; the time of year; your current financial condition; whether you are the incumbent; the current market, pricing, and demand for your product or service; and any emerging competitors. Only by doing so will you be able to construct a clear and accurate picture of the situation.

Finally, it's important to bear in mind that what you are doing in this step of the process is making estimates—essentially educated guesses, based on what you've learned from past deals and from the sales process, about your customer's business and industry. At this point you cannot, nor are you expected to, know with certainty what the other side's Consequence of No Agreement will actually be. Later on I show you how to gather information from others in your own organization, as well as from outside sources, to validate the estimates you are making here.

Once you've gathered the information you need to determine the other side's Consequences of No Agreement and its short-term and long-term effects, it's advantageous to record that information in the format shown on page 59.

•　•　•　•　•

Now that you've analyzed and recorded the Consequences of No Agreement and costs and benefits associated with those consequences for both sides in your own negotiation, it's time to put them together so you can apply them. As promised in the beginning of the chapter, having gathered this information you will now be able to answer the two questions that will enable you to take your first step toward becoming a world-class negotiator: "Who has the power in the negotiation?" and "Where is the Agreement Zone?" Just to give you an idea of how it's done, here are the two lists of costs and benefits I used for the sample negotiation.

CONSEQUENCES OF NO AGREEMENT—THE OTHER SIDE

1. Their most likely Consequence of No Agreement is: _____
   _____

2. The short-term and long-term hard costs associated with that Consequence of No Agreement are: _____
   _____
   _____
   _____
   _____
   _____

3. The short-term and long-term soft costs associated with that Consequence of No Agreement are: _____
   _____
   _____
   _____
   _____
   _____

4. The short-term and long-term hard benefits associated with that Consequence of No Agreement are: _____
   _____
   _____
   _____
   _____
   _____

5. The short-term and long-term soft benefits associated with that Consequence of No Agreement are: _____
   _____
   _____
   _____
   _____
   _____

6. The data we still need about the above is: _____
   _____
   _____
   _____
   _____

The Seller's Consequence of No Agreement: Losing the Sale

Elements to Be Considered	Cost/Benefit
$100,000 in revenue; costs of sale; my bonus	*Hard Cost*
My boss will not be happy; competitors will get my customer	*Soft Cost*
Market price is 4 percent higher than the client is willing to pay	*Hard Benefit*
The client was very tough on our operations team	*Soft Benefit*

The Buyer's Consequence of No Agreement: Going to a Competitor

Elements to Be Considered	Cost/Benefit
Higher long-term maintenance; higher switching costs; lower output	*Hard Cost*
Hassle of retraining staff	*Soft Cost*
Competitor's price is 9 percent lower in the short term	*Hard Benefit*
Will be a more important client to my competitor than he or she is to me	*Soft Benefit*

Determining Who Has the Power

Now let's look again at the first of the two questions: Who has the power in the negotiation? Determining the answer to this question is important because it affects how both sides think of the negotiation and, as a result, how they behave. Those who think they have more power in the negotiation tend to *overestimate* the value of their offer. As a result, they're more likely to play hardball in the negotiation and are less willing to consider making trades. And when either side is unwilling to make trades, it makes creating value difficult for both sides and increases the likelihood of impasse. On the other hand, those who think they have less power are likely to *underestimate* the value of their offer, are likely to roll over too easily, and, in the process, unnecessarily give up value to the other side.

Interestingly, our experience has taught us that both sellers and buyers are likely to misdiagnose who has the power. They both tend to think that the other side has more power in any given situation. For example, a seller we worked with recently told us that a customer had them "over a barrel" in a negotiation. The seller was providing data services to a major telecom company and had been told by the buyer that, although they had been the only seller in the market, there were now two other suppliers with exactly the same data. In fact, one of those competitors had offered to not only discount their fees by almost 50 percent but also to pay both the cost of taking the existing data out of the customer's organization and the cost of switching suppliers.

In the meantime, the seller's account manager was being pushed on her sales goals for the year and was afraid that her job might be in jeopardy if she lost this high-visibility account. In other words, her Consequences of No Agreement weren't very good. She felt, understandably, that the customer had all the power in this negotiation and that she could lose the sale if she didn't concede. If she gave in, she reasoned, at least her company would retain the business, even if at a much lower margin.

When we completed the Consequences of No Agreement Estimation for both sides in this situation, however, we realized several things. First, the data the competitor was offering the telecom company wasn't actually the same as our client's data. When we compared our client's data with its competitor's, we found that the competitor could provide only domestic data, while our client had been providing global data. We also found that the buyer had just invested in a quarter-million-dollar system to integrate the existing supplier's data into several key global databases, a system that would be rendered useless if the existing supplier were replaced. Finally, we recognized that taking the client's data out of the buyer's system—which the competitor had promised to do—would be a large, complex, and very expensive task. Although it was possible that the new supplier might have been able to assume some of the cost, it would be unrealistic to believe they could—or would—pay for all of it.

In other words, we were able to show that the buyer had not done complete due diligence, had only a verbal offer from our client's competitor, and was misinformed about that competitor's capabilities. Adding to this the potential risks of using a new, unproven supplier, the question of how much of the switching costs the supplier would actually cover and the new system the buyer had just installed, it became clear that our client had considerably more power in the negotiation than they thought they did.

On the other hand, we recently worked with a *buyer*—a major U.S. airline—who told us that the seller had *it* "over a barrel" in a negotiation. The airline was in the process of renewing its deal with a ground services provider in a very popular European destination. But it was frustrated by the fact that the provider was owned by the government and there were no alternative suppliers. The seller told the airline that "plenty of other carriers were willing to accept your gates" and they'd either have to agree to the supplier's terms or pull out of the market, which would then be the airline's Consequence of No Agreement. The airline felt it couldn't afford to lose this critical vacation and business destination, so the airline's buyer had been told to get the deal done. Their thinking was that even if their costs went up 30 or even 40 percent—hundreds of thousands of dollars—it would still be less than the millions they would lose if they accepted their Consequence of No Agreement and pulled out of the market. They felt, in other words, that they had no choice but to agree to the seller's terms.

Again, however, when we did the Consequences of No Agreement Estimation for both sides in the negotiation, we found that the situation was not actually what it appeared to be. For one thing, although not reaching an agreement could very seriously damage the airline, it would be almost equally devastating for the city. This particular city relied on the airline for a major portion of both its tourists and business travelers. If the airline pulled out, even if it was replaced by another major airline, tourists who wanted to use frequent-flyer miles to get there would be greatly inconvenienced and might well choose other destinations. So too might people who preferred using this airline to get to the city but would be unable to because the airline no longer flew there.

Fewer tourists and business travelers would, in turn, mean the loss of jobs, which would create problems with the airport workers' unions as well as incur political ramifications for the city's leaders. In addition, although the city said other carriers were interested in filling our client's gates, in reality, making such arrangements would be both time consuming and costly. In other words, even though the buyer felt that the seller had all the power in the negotiation, that wasn't really true.

As you can see from these scenarios, both buyers and sellers can be mistaken in believing that the other side has all the power in a negotiation. Conducting the Consequences of No Agreement Estimation enables you to determine what it would mean to both sides if no agreement is reached and provides you with an understanding of the power you have as well as the power your customer has. Had both the buyer and seller in these examples conducted their own Consequences of No Agreement Estimation for both sides, they would have recognized they both had at least some power in the negotiation—and usually more than they had initially thought.

So who has more power in your own negotiation situation, you or the other side? All the information you've developed and recorded may have made it clear that you have much more power than you thought you did. If that's the case, then doing the estimation will clearly have benefited you by enabling you to negotiate from a position of strength.

Conversely, the estimation may have shown that you don't have as much power as you believed. In that case, you will still have benefited from it because it will have allowed you to see and recognize your limitations. At the same time, it will enable you to determine if there is anything you can do about the situation. When my partner Max's cousin thoroughly analyzed his own Consequences of No Agreement while negotiating to buy a house, he recognized that the consequences were not necessarily what he'd anticipated, and he was able to change his Consequences of No Agreement for the better.

Max and I found ourselves in a similar situation when we first started our firm. In those days it was just Max, me, the dog, and the kitchen table. We had one lead—a major U.S. insurance company—and knew that if we lost the business (our Consequence of No Agreement), we could be in financial trouble because we had no other customers (the effect of our Consequence of No Agreement). Naturally, we recognized while we were negotiating with this firm that we had very little power. But having recognized that, we were able to do something about it. We began spending more time prospecting for additional customers, which not only enabled us to make money but, even more important, make our Consequences of No Agreement a bit better, and thus increase our power in negotiations.

Whether you've determined that you have more power than you thought or that your customer does, it's advantageous to record what you believe to be true:

Based on my preliminary Consequences of No Agreement Estimation of this negotiation, I believe:
1. I have more power. _____
2. The other side has more power. _____
3. I still don't know. _____

Finding the Agreement Zone

As noted earlier, conducting a Consequences of No Agreement Estimation enables you to determine both who has the power in the negotiation and the place where both sides prefer agreement to impasse. Now that you've learned more about whether it's you or the other side that has more power in your own negotiating situation, giving you a clear picture of who stands where, it's time to figure out where you and those on the other side can meet: the Agreement Zone.

The concept of an Agreement Zone comes from the pioneering work of Roger Fisher and William L. Ury in their 1981 book *Getting to Yes*, which first advanced the idea of "win-win" as a negotiating strategy. "Win-win" was a substantial improvement over the old school of thinking about negotiation, which might have been described as "I win–you lose," or vice versa. Fisher and Ury made it clear that the only time you reach a good business agreement ("win-win") is when both sides are in positions in which they are better off than they would have been if they hadn't agreed. This position, or place, is the Agreement Zone, or, as one of our clients from Japan calls it, the "sweet spot."

But what exactly is this sweet spot, and how do you find it? Here's a simple example. A company has a product that's been selling very well at an average market price of $12 per unit. The company has a customer in the same town that wants to buy the product. The customer can, however, get the product from another supplier for $11, which is then the customer's—oversimplified—Consequence of No Agreement. But because the other supplier is in another town, the customer would also have to pay for shipping at $3 per unit. The buyer's true Consequence of No Agreement, then, is $14, and the seller's is $12. The Agreement Zone, or sweet spot, is $2. So as long as the buyer is willing to pay at least $12 for the product, the seller's Consequence of No Agreement, and the

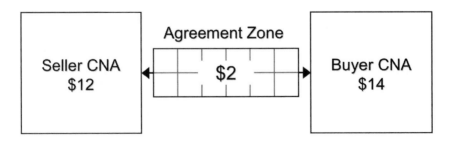

seller is willing to accept less than $14, the buyer's Consequence of No Agreement, both sides come out better than they would if they hadn't made the deal.

This example also demonstrates that you should accept any offer, even if you don't like it, so long as it's better than your Consequence of No Agreement. Let's say, for example, that I tell you I'm going to give you and your best friend $100. Your friend will be able to decide how to divide the money between you, but you both have to agree on that distribution before I hand it over. The easy solution would be to share the money evenly because that's "fair." But what if, instead, your friend wants to keep $95 for herself and give you $5? How likely are you to take that deal? Most likely, you'll decline. But is that really the best strategy? If you refuse the deal, you get the Consequence of No Agreement—zero dollars. If you accept, you get $5, which is clearly better than your Consequence of No Agreement.

The point here is that in trying to find the Agreement Zone, it's important for you to remember that you are not in competition with your customer. Your customer's success has little to do with your evaluation of the deal. Even if the customer is going to come away from this particular negotiation with gobs of money, you should take the deal as long as you can do better than your Consequence of No Agreement. The only real issue, then, is exactly what your Consequence of No Agreement is. And as you've now seen, you can only determine that through the Consequences of No Agreement Estimation you've just conducted. More important, though, as you will see in the following chapters, is that you will actually be able to enlarge the Agreement Zone by conducting this kind of analysis. In other words, you'll actually be able to grow that sweet spot from $2 to $3, $4, or even $5 so that both you and your customer will be able to come away with a better deal than either of you could have anticipated going into it.

Best Practices Review

- Complete Consequences of No Agreement Estimations for each deal. Despite many similarities, every deal is unique in some way and must be considered on its own to attain an accurate estimation.

- Be as honest as possible about both sides' Consequences of No Agreements. Facts, not opinions, are what you're looking for here.
- Take a deal as long as it's better than your Consequence of No Agreement . . . even if you don't like it.

Common Mistakes to Avoid

- Overstating the disadvantages of your own Consequence of No Agreement and the advantages of your customer's
- Confusing the Consequence of No Agreement with its costs and benefits. Losing the business is a Consequence of No Agreement. Losing $100,000 is a cost.
- Trying to sell the value of your offer before you can show how it's better than the other side's Consequences of No Agreement

• • • • •

The Consequences of No Agreement Estimation is the first of two parts of the first step in the Strategic Negotiation Process. Having now conducted that analysis, having determined what effects not reaching an agreement will have on both you and your customer, and having determined who has the power in the negotiation in addition to the place where both sides prefer agreement to impasse, it's time to go on to the second part, the Wish List Estimation.

5

STEP ONE
ESTIMATING THE BLUEPRINT

PART TWO
The Wish List Estimation

Having now completed the first part of Step One: Estimating the Blueprint—the Consequences of No Agreement Estimation—it's time to go on to the second part—the Wish List Estimation.

Estimate	Validate	Create Value	Divide Value
⊕ CNA ⊕ **Wish List of Trades**	⊕ In-House/Public Sources ⊕ Meeting Preparation ⊕ Validation Meeting	⊕ Exceed CNAs ⊕ Look for Trades	⊕ Anchor on MEO ⊕ Trading ⊕ Claim Value

Again, the overall purpose of this step is to determine the blueprint of the business deal, which means, in effect, answering two questions: "What are the consequences if we do not reach agreement?" and "What items are likely to be included if we do reach agreement?" The Consequences of No Agreement Estimation provided you with an answer to the first question. The Wish List Estimation begins to provide you with an answer to the second by enabling you to determine what is most—and least—important to you and your customer. It also shows what both of you will trade, or should be willing to trade, to attain your goal to "create joint value and divide it given concerns for fairness in the ongoing relationship." This is an essential part of the process because trading—giving up something in order to gain something of greater value—is the soul of negotiation and of the Strategic Negotiation Process. It's what enables you to create more value to subsequently divide between yourself and your customer and achieve more than a simple "win-win" solution.

CREATING VALUE

You should bear in mind three very important rules in regard to creating value in a negotiation. The first concerns the meaning of value itself, which is expressed as *Value = Benefit – Cost*. We've all, of course, heard about sales processes that are supposed to add value but hardly ever succeed in creating real, measurable business value. The Strategic Negotiation Process does succeed, though, because it enables you to add "hard" value (value you can measure) rather than "soft" value. If you can't put a potential trade through the equation above, you're not creating value. The second rule is: *Never concede—always trade.* If you simply concede on an item during a negotiation, you are eliminating the possibility of creating value because value is created by trading items that have differing importance to the two sides in a negotiation. The third rule is: *Never negotiate one thing by itself.* If you negotiate one item at a time, you will soon find that you don't have any other items with which to trade, and if you can't trade, you can't create value.

Creating value is, of course, something that has to work for both you and your customer, or it doesn't work for either of you. Salespeople like yourself have two very good reasons to embrace the concept of value creation. First, it makes it easier for you to negotiate with buyers because it's easier to divide a larger pie than a smaller one. And, second, it enables you to make more money by providing you with the ability to make bigger deals, and over time bigger deals mean more money. However, even though creating a larger pie and a bigger deal is ultimately beneficial to both sides in a negotiation, buyers don't necessarily see it that way. Because, as a rule, buyers are primarily interested in lower prices, they're less likely than you to be concerned about value-creating trades. And that's why it's often incumbent on you—the seller—to show the buyer how and why creating value can be advantageous to both of you.

As a matter of fact, I was in just such a position myself a few years ago. As I've mentioned, I own, and live in, a building with several rental apartments, and when one of my tenants moved out, I needed to find another to replace him. The outgoing tenant had been paying $1,000 a month—the going rate for a two-bedroom in Chicago—and I wanted to get at least as much from a new tenant. Now a rent negotiation would appear to be a "zero-sum" sort of negotiation—one in which one side loses and the other wins, or, at best, you arrive at a "win-win" solution. For example, if I asked a prospective tenant for $1,000, he said he'd only pay $900, and I accepted it, the tenant would have gained $100 and I would have lost $100. All we would have done was "rearrange" value—a zero-sum, win-lose approach.

Let's say, though, that I'm asking $1,000 a month for the apartment and the prospective tenant can only afford $900, but we agree that the tenant will clean the hallways in return for a $100 discount on the rent. I'm already paying $100 a month for a cleaning service, so by trading for having the hall cleaned by the tenant I'm still getting $1,000 in value, and the tenant is getting the apartment for what he can afford. This is a "win-win" solution. Still, as in the first scenario, although we would have reached an agreement, all we would have done was rearrange value, not create it. But because I wanted something else from a new tenant, I wanted to devise a value-creating deal, so I placed an ad for the apartment that read as follows: "Beautiful, remodeled, 2 BR, 1.5 bath vintage apartment. Hardwood floors. Fireplace. Rent of $1,100 per month with no dog and $1,000 per month with a dog."

The first few people who called about the apartment said that they didn't have dogs and that, as there was obviously a mistake in the ad, they assumed they'd only have to pay $1,000. When I told them that the ad was right, they asked why, to which I replied, "You wouldn't understand." The next call that came in was from some people who did have a dog. They said they were interested in the apartment, but because they also thought there was an error in the ad, understood they'd have to pay $1,100 a month. "No," I said, "you get the lower rent." Although they said they'd take the apartment sight unseen, they were also—understandably—curious about why the rent was lower. "I've got a dog myself,"

I explained, "an Alaskan Malamute. As you know, Malamutes are pack dogs, and he could use a playmate. Having another dog in the building would be great." Of course, providing a playmate for my dog didn't cost the new tenants anything. It did, though, provide me with great value, not to mention the value to my dog. In other words, by trading we had created value in the negotiation.

In fact, we subsequently negotiated an even better arrangement for both of us. It turned out that the new tenants owned a mobile dog grooming business called "Shampooch." At the time, I was paying $85 a month to have my dog picked up, groomed, and brought home. I learned, though, that it actually only cost my new tenants about $20 to groom a dog. So we agreed that, in return for grooming my dog every month, I'd lower their rent by an additional $50. This trade created $35 of value for me ($85–$50) at the same time that it lowered my income (their rent) by $50. It also created $30 of value for them ($50–$20) while lowering their rent.

Of course, in this instance we weren't talking about a lot of money. The point is, though, that regardless of how much money is involved, world-class negotiators always look for trades like these that actually provide both sides with more than they were originally looking for. Although from a mathematical perspective it doesn't seem possible, it is, in fact, eminently possible, as this example shows. Of course, even though I was the seller in this situation, that doesn't mean that *only* a seller can create value in a negotiation. There have been many examples of situations in which buyers have presented sellers with value-creating trades. One of my favorite examples comes from Henry Ford. As legend has it, Ford was negotiating the purchase of door handles for his Model T with his usual supplier. The supplier was asking for a 5 percent increase in the price that Ford, understandably, didn't want to pay. As a result, they appeared to be at an impasse. The carmaker, however, thought of a way out.

At the time, the door handles came to the Ford plant packed in wooden crates. Ford told the supplier he could have his 5 percent increase if he'd agree to change the size and location of the bolt holes on the lids of the wooden crates. Because it would cost him virtually nothing to make the change, the supplier was happy to do it. Ford was happy as well because, as it happened, the floorboards of the Model Ts were also made of wood, and with the modification, Ford was able to use the crate lids as floorboards. The trade did, of course, increase Ford's cost for the handles, but that increase was far outweighed by the savings he realized by eliminating the cost of raw materials and the processing of the floorboards.

Another example of a buyer creating value comes from an experience we had with one of our clients. The client, an insurance company, was negotiating with the commercial sellers at a large retail home improvement firm for the purchase of carpet to use for the damage claims of its policyholders. The lead item being negotiated was, of course, price per yard. The buyer kept leveraging the volume in an effort to lower the unit cost, while the seller continued to tout the carpet's quality in order to maintain the price. They attempted to trade warehousing, just-in-time inventory, payment terms, and length of contract, all to no avail. The negotiators on both sides were professionals who were well-versed in big-ticket negotiation, but enough business value wasn't being created despite their best efforts to offset the gap in pricing both sides wanted. And then the buyer, not the seller, got creative.

Using the Strategic Negotiation Process, the buyer—the insurance company—began to look for trades beyond the obvious ones and after considerable thought came up with one. At the time, the buyer was preparing to purchase data about a specific section of consumers from a data management firm. As it happened, though, the seller—the home improvement firm—had the same data. So for the moment, the price per yard of carpeting was set aside, and the two companies reached an agreement that allowed them to "trade tapes," that is, to marry their consumer databases. The cost to the supplier was zero; the value to the buyer was immense. But the trade not only reduced costs for the buyer, it also allowed both sides to realize a revenue opportunity, as they used the new joint database for consumer-marketing programs.

There are several morals, if you will, to these stories. The first is that both sides benefit when value is created, regardless of whether it's the seller or the buyer who comes up with the trade. The second is that even in a simple business deal, it's actually very easy to find ways to create value. And the third is that in more complex business negotiations, when there are more things that can be discussed between the two sides, there are even more opportunities to create value. If you're like me, after a while it becomes a personal challenge to turn any apparently single-item, zero-sum, concession-oriented negotiation into a multiple-item, value-creating negotiation.

THE WISH LIST ESTIMATION

Before you can even begin to think about trading, though, you must first determine what both you and your customer want out of the negotiation—what we call a Wish List. Oddly enough, we often find that people have no clear idea of what they're looking for. This is often true on the buyer's side, particularly when a buyer is negotiating on behalf of several people, and they haven't gotten together to figure out what they all want. And needless to say, if you don't know what you're looking for, it's difficult to find it. Of course, buyers who give little thought to what they themselves expect from a negotiation are likely to give even less thought to what their suppliers might expect. As a result, they are often amazed by the demands made by the other side, even though the sellers may have been asking for the same things for years. In fact, it's exactly the absence of a clear understanding of what's being negotiated that so often makes negotiations a tactical, emotion-driven mess, with the erratic tactics of one side countering the erratic tactics of the other. In other words, it's not the personalities of the players that cause problems, but rather the lack of a clear plan driven by a clear goal.

The Wish List Estimation is designed to help you avoid that mess. It does so by enabling you to answer four essential questions for yourself and for your customer:

1. What items do you wish to be part of the final deal?
2. Which of these items are the most important?
3. How should these items be weighted relative to each other?
4. What are the high and low ranges for these items (i.e., how many and how few of each item, how long and how short should each be, etc.)?

Only when you can answer all of these questions with a high degree of accuracy will you be ready to negotiate. Of course, at this point you'll find it much easier to answer these questions for yourself than for your customer. Your estimation of what the other side wants is likely to be full of blanks right now, again partly because several people are likely to be involved on the other side, and they don't know themselves! That is not, however, a problem; in fact, it's to be expected, and later on I show you how to fill in those blanks. In light of that, though, as I did with the Consequences of No Agreement, I'll begin the Wish List Estimation with your side of the negotiation.

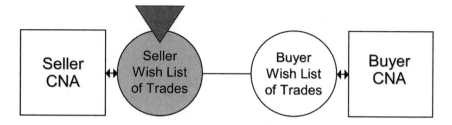

Your Side's Wish List Estimation

Ultimately, when you've concluded the Wish List Estimation for your side, you will know the items that you want included in the final deal, their ranking and weight relative to each other, and the range from highest to lowest for each. Just to give you a better idea of what I'm talking about, here's an example:

	Typical Seller Wish List Estimation		
Rank	*Item*	*Weight*	*Range (High to Low)*
1.	Length of contract	40%	3–1 years
2.	Volume	25%	3–1,000 units
3.	Price	15%	$20–$16
4.	Payment terms	10%	30–45 days
5.	Service	10%	8/5–24/7

In conducting the Wish List Estimation, however, you should take into consideration several things. Among the most important are the concerns of other individuals on your side of the negotiation. For that reason, you should talk to people in your legal department, in product management, in pricing, and anyone else in your organization who has a stake in whatever deal you make to find out what they're looking for. If you don't know what they want, it's going to be very difficult to make a deal that will be acceptable to them. In fact, you're much more likely to be successful in getting them to approve the deal if you get their input early on in the negotiating process than if you go to the customer, secure an agreement, and then come back and ask people in your organization to accept it.

What items do you wish to be part of the final deal? As noted above, the first question you have to answer is "What items do you wish to be part of the final deal?" As you'll see, the answers to this question generally speaking don't vary very much from one negotiation to another. That is, sellers are usually concerned about the same items, as are buyers, regardless of what's being sold. These typically include volume, price, length of contract, payment terms, and service. There may, however, be others that you would like to have included in this negotiation. You may, for example, be currently negotiating for a customer's business in Canada but would also like to have its Latin American business. Similarly, you may be trying to sell your product into a different division of your customer's company or sell your current customer a new product. Even though such items may not be on the table at this point, you should put them on the list anyway, as you might be able to trade something else to get them later on. Remember that the more items you include on the list, the more potential trades you will have.

Which of these items are the most important? Before you start to list the items that you want to include in the final deal, you should stop for a moment and think about which are the most important. Unlike the answers to the first question—which tend to be the same regardless of the specifics of the deal—the answers to this question may vary. For example, in the previous Typical Seller Wish List Estimation, the seller is most concerned with length of contract and volume, listing them as first and second in importance. If, however, the seller were experiencing a cash flow problem at the time they were negotiating this deal, they might place more importance on payment terms and price and put those at the top of their list.

Ranking the importance of the items to be negotiated is a vital aspect of the Wish List Estimation for several reasons. First, it's the fact that not every item is equally important to both sides in a negotiation that provides an opportunity to make value-creating trades. Second, customers tend to say that everything is equally important, so doing the ranking enables you to get beyond that to discover what really is important. And, finally, listing the items in their order of importance forces you to recognize what you absolutely must have and what you can do without.

How should these items be weighted relative to each other? Having determined what items are most to least important to you, the next step is to determine how much weight each should be given. That is, if all the items together add up to 100 percent, what percentage would you assign to each? In the Typical Seller Wish List Estimation above, for example, length of contract, the most important item, was assigned 40 percent, while the other items were assigned smaller amounts. This is an important part of the Wish List Estimation because, again, it's the difference in importance that you and your customer place on these items that will enable you to make value-creating trades.

What are the high and low ranges for these items (i.e., how many and how few of each item, how long and how short should each be, etc.)? Finally, to give you as clear as possible an idea of how much you will be willing, or can afford, to trade, it's essential that you provide a metric range for each of the items on your list. These can be dollars, percentages, days, hours, people, yes/no, or whatever so long as they are measurable. As you can see in the Typical Seller Wish List Estimation, the range for "Volume" is listed as "3–1,000 units." Similarly, the range for price is listed as "$20–$16." Attaching a metric to each item is essential because, unless you do, you have no way of measuring whether you are getting what you wanted.

Creating a range is equally important because it provides you with flexibility when you are making trades. With a range of acceptable outcomes, you have the ability to trade down on one item in exchange for something more important. There are several options for trades here, for example: adding new items to the Wish List, taking out items you don't need and the other side wants out, or taking the low end of the range for one item in exchange for the high end on another.

Now think about your own negotiation and make a Wish List for your side in the space on page 76.

The Other Side's Wish List Estimation

Having completed the Wish List Estimation for your side, it's now time to do the same for your customer.

WISH LIST ESTIMATION

Our Side

Rank	Item	Weight	Range (High to Low)
1.			
2.			
3.			
4.			
5.			
6.			
7.			
8.			

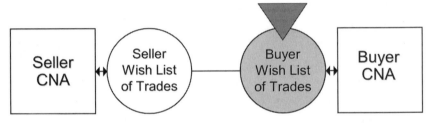

As with the Consequences of No Agreement, it's considerably easier at this point to figure out what you want than it is to figure out what the people across the table may want. But that doesn't mean you can't determine anything about the other side. If you've made deals with this customer in the past, you should have a pretty good idea of what they'll be looking for. Even if you haven't concluded any deals with them before, it's likely that you learned a great deal about them during the sales process. And that knowledge is exactly what you should be focusing on at this point in the negotiation. In fact, you probably know pretty much what they want, although you're probably less sure about ranking, weights, and ranges. If you don't know the answers to these questions, that's fine. Put a question mark next to the things you're not sure about, and you'll use those question marks to guide you when you get to the validation stage.

As with the Wish List Estimation you did for your own side, when you've concluded the estimation for your customer you'll know the items that he or she wants included in the final deal, their ranking and weight relative to each other, and the range for each from highest to lowest. Again, to give you a better idea of the end result, here's an example.

Typical Buyer Wish List Estimation			
Rank	Item	Weight	Range (High to Low)
1.	Price	40%	$14–$18
2.	Payment terms	20%	60–45 days
3.	Service	20%	24/7 – 12/7
4.	Length of contract	10%	0–2 years
5.	Volume	10%	1–2,000 units

What items do they wish to be part of the final deal? As I've noted, what the buyer wants in a typical deal doesn't vary a great deal from one negotiation to another. As with the seller, the items that are usually important to a buyer include length of contract, volume, price, payment terms, and service. Again, however, at this point it's also advantageous to think about other items that aren't currently included in this negotiation, items that your customer might be interested in, such as purchasing another one of your company's products or purchasing your product for another division of his or her company. The more items on the table, the more potential there is for trades.

Which of these items are the most important? The next question you have to answer is how important these items are to your customer. The customer in the Typical Buyer Wish List Estimation above was like many, if not most, buyers most interested in price, while payment terms, service, and other items were of less importance. It's likely that you'll have a good idea from the sales process which items are most important to your customer, but again you can put question marks next to items you're not sure of and come back to them in the validation stage.

How should these items be weighted relative to each other? As with the Wish List Estimation you did for your own side, the next question you have to answer about your customer is how much weight he or she places on each of the items on the list. Again looking back at the Typical Buyer Wish List Estimation, you can see that the buyer in that situation considered his most important item, price, to represent 40 percent of the total and assigning lesser amounts to payment terms, service, length of contract, and volume. Estimating how important each of these items is to your customer is essential, because it's the difference in how important they are to you and to him that will enable you to make value-creating trades. Of course, you can't know precisely how much weight your customer will place on these items—in all likelihood, they don't know themselves—but you can estimate them at this point. Later on, I show you how you can confirm those estimates.

What are the high and low ranges for these items (i.e., how many and how few of each item, how long and how short should each be, etc.)? Finally, as you did in your own Wish List Estimation, to determine how much your customer will be willing, or can afford, to trade, you have to provide a metric range for each item on the list. Again, these can be dollars, percentages, days, hours, people, or anything else that can be represented by numbers. In the Typical Buyer Wish List Estimation, for example, the range for price is listed as "$14–$18" and that for length of contract is listed as "0–2 years." Attaching a metric to each item on your customer's Wish List is indispensable because you and your customer need a common metric in order to trade. For example, if your customer is measuring by using the total cost of all units purchased and you are measuring by using unit price, you will have to establish a common metric in order to measure the trade. If you can't measure it, you can't trade it, and if you can't trade it, you can't measure its value!

Now, go back to your own negotiation and make a Wish List for your customer in the space on page 79.

Using the Wish List Estimation

Your initial analysis won't look as "clean" as the samples above, which represent a complete analysis, one for which any and all questions have been answered. At this point you'll probably have more blank spaces than filled-in ones, particularly in the analysis of your customer. It is, nevertheless, a good place to start. Bear in mind that this is a process and that the following chapters show you how to tighten up your analysis and fill in all the blanks. In addition, as you become more accustomed to

---

WISH LIST ESTIMATION

The Other Side

Rank Item	Weight	Range (High to Low)
1. _____	_____	_____
2. _____	_____	_____
3. _____	_____	_____
4. _____	_____	_____
5. _____	_____	_____
6. _____	_____	_____
7. _____	_____	_____
8. _____	_____	_____

---

doing the analysis, you'll find that you can actually fill in more and more of the information even at this stage.

Even in its incomplete state, an analysis like the one you've just performed accomplishes a number of things. Perhaps the most obvious, if not the most important, is that it enables you to become organized. As I mentioned at the beginning of this chapter, if you don't know what you want, it's difficult to go after it. Performing this analysis enables you to determine what you and all those in your organization with a stake in the deal want—and in very clear terms.

The analysis also enables you to help the other side organize itself. I've seen many instances in which customers appear to be playing hardball because they keep coming back to ask for more and more. Sometimes, of course, they *are* playing hardball. But as often as not, the reason they keep coming back is that they haven't done this kind of analysis themselves, and it's only when they've discussed an almost finalized deal with their boss or some other stakeholder in the company that they discover exactly what that individual expects to get out of the deal. By conducting a Wish List Estimation for yourself as well as for your customers, you can take charge of the negotiation and manage it to help them achieve what they want by trading for items that are important to you. World-class negotiators actually help both themselves and those on the other side to get as much of their Wish List as possible.

Most important, doing this kind of analysis, as you've seen, not only enables you to develop a list of items that can be used to trade with your customer but also shows you which of those items present the best opportunities for trades. Look again at the Typical Seller and Typical Buyer Wish List Estimations, concentrating this time on the differences in importance in weighting and in metrics.

Typical Seller Wish List Estimation

Rank	Item	Weight	Range (High to Low)
1.	Length of contract	40%	3–1 years
2.	Volume	25%	3–1,000 units
3.	Price	15%	$20–$16
4.	Payment terms	10%	30–45 days
5.	Service	10%	8/5 – 24/7

Typical Buyer Wish List Estimation

Rank	Item	Weight	Range (High to Low)
1.	Price	40%	$14–$18
2.	Payment terms	20%	60–45 days
3.	Service	20%	24/7 – 12/7
4.	Length of contract	10%	0–2 years
5.	Volume	10%	1–2,000 units

As you can see here, by showing the extent to which you and your customer place differing importance on the various items on the list, the Wish List Estimation provides you with information and enables you to find those value-creating trades to expand the Agreement Zone.

DEALING WITH Professional Buyers

Many sellers continue to believe that buyers are only interested in low price. But almost any business-to-business sale in which a professional buyer is involved is likely to be a complex one with multiple criteria to be met on both sides, and buyers are certainly aware of that. Let's start by looking at the kind of CNA Estimation you need to do when dealing with professional buyers. The following list of supplier performance metrics is from "The Supplier Selection and Management Report 9/01" from the National Association of Purchasing Managers (now the Institute of Supply Management).

- Financial stability
- People
- Supplier performance
- Supplier cost reduction ideas
- Supplier development projects
- Delivery
- Quality
- Product cost
- Order accuracy
- Customer support
- Business relations

These are the things that buyers themselves use for analyzing their Consequences of No Agreement, and, as you can see, not only is price not the primary concern but it's number eight on the list! Perhaps even more important, the list shows that professional buyers are concerned about the same kind of CNA issues that we've been discussing.

The story is pretty much the same for Wish List items. Most professional supply managers act on behalf of an internal customer and/or user group, and it's these individuals who help the supply manager determine the Wish List items that will be negotiated in the deal. For example, someone sourcing technology for a production facility is likely to receive input from the vice president of manufacturing, technicians on the manufacturing floor, and the vice president of technology, as well as from people in other affected departments, such as accounting. And those individuals are likely to want the buyer to concern himself or herself with price, length of contract, volume of purchase, which add-ons or value additions to purchase, warranty issues, and support issues—again, the same kind of Wish List items we've been talking about.

The point here is that professional buyers know even better what they want than do nonprofessionals and are subject to even more pressure because they're acting on behalf of others. Given that, it only makes sense that in negotiating a deal you should do all you can to help a supply manager achieve as many of his or her internal customer objectives as possible, while at the same time trading for items of importance to you.

B *est* **P** *ractices* **R** *eview*

- Consult multiple stakeholders in your organization to list and pri-
oritize your own Wish List.
- Push yourself hard to generate ideas for trades beyond the main
item in the negotiation.
- Look for creative trades to broaden the negotiation beyond
what's on the table now. Look for the floorboards!
- Determine the value of items the customer sees as "free" or
needed just to be considered so you can trade them rather than
give them away.

C *ommon* **M** *istakes to* **A** *void*

- Trying to trade something without measuring it. Find a metric for
each trade, such as people, dollars, percentages, days, and the
like. If you can't measure it, you can't trade it.
- Thinking of "quality" or other similar elements as something you
can trade. Quality is a Consequences of No Agreement issue, not
a Wish List one.
- Overlooking the ranking of Wish List items for both sides. It's the
gap between rankings on the two sides that creates opportunities
for trades.

· · · · ·

You have now taken the first step toward blueprinting your business
deal by developing a goal to "create joint value and divide it given concerns for fairness in the ongoing relationship" and conducting Consequences of No Agreement and Wish List Estimations for both sides in
the negotiation. In the next step of the process you conduct a fact-finding
exercise designed to enable you to validate the results of the "best guess"
analyses you've just completed.

6

STEP TWO
VALIDATING THE
ESTIMATION

PART ONE

Gathering Data from Colleagues and Public Sources

Now that you've completed the estimating step of blueprinting your negotiation, it's time to go on to Step Two: Validating the Estimation.

Estimate	Validate	Create Value	Divide Value
⊕ CNA	⊕ **In-House/Public Sources**	⊕ Exceed CNAs	⊕ Anchor on MEO
⊕ Wish List of Trades	⊕ Meeting Preparation	⊕ Look for Trades	⊕ Trading
	⊕ Validation Meeting		⊕ Claim Value

The estimation you made in the first step was based on your own knowledge—of yourself and of your customer. That estimation essentially enabled you to begin to answer the question "What are the consequences if we do not reach agreement?" But there were—unavoidably—gaps in that answer, primarily about your customer, that have to be filled in if you want to conduct successful negotiations. In this second step, then, you identify what information you still need and gather that information from three different sources: (1) others in your organization, (2) publicly available data, and (3) your customer. Doing so enables you to answer the second question you need to answer: "What items are likely to be included if we do reach agreement?" This chapter concentrates on the first two sources of information—others in your organization and publicly available data—and the next two chapters on preparing for a validation meeting with your customer.

IT'S ALL ABOUT KNOWLEDGE

The single most important element in any negotiation is *knowledge,* so it's essential to have as much data—and accurate data—as possible. At the same time, I recognize that going through the estimation and validation steps can seem to be very time consuming. In fact, some of our clients tell us that they don't have time to do them, and we understand that. My advice, then, is simply to spend as much time as you have. If you need to respond to a customer within 15 minutes, spend 15 minutes on these steps. If you have hours, days, or weeks to respond, as you might for a large and important negotiation, use that time. In other words, spend as much time on these steps as the negotiation warrants and time allows. Even a little time is better than none.

For example, I once received a lengthy request for proposal (RFP) from a major U.S. airline. After reading through it, I did a quick estimation (the first step of the process), then phoned the client to ask a few validation questions. Once I got my answers (the second step), I was about to hang up when the client abruptly asked me for my proposal, right then, on the phone. After I caught my breath, I asked if he'd hold on for five minutes. While he was holding, I used my preliminary estimations and validations to create value (the third step), presented my offers (the fourth step), and closed the deal on the phone. Although at this point it may seem impossible to you to blueprint a negotiation so quickly, the fact is that once you've done it a few times, it becomes second nature, so you actually can do it "on the fly."

Taking the time to validate the Consequences of No Agreement (CNA) and Wish List Estimations serves several purposes. The most important of these is that it enables you to organize the negotiation both for yourself and for your customer so that you can proactively manage the process rather than react tactically—that is, emotionally—to it. In addition, because more often than not your customers won't have taken the time to even make estimates, much less validate them, you'll know more about their CNA and Wish List than they do, which puts you in the driver's seat in the negotiation. And because that's true even if you spend only 15 minutes thinking through their position, you can imagine how advantageous it can be if you devote more time to it.

Another benefit of validating your estimations is that it helps you to be objective and rational in conducting the negotiation. That's because the more accurate data you have, the easier it is to maintain objectivity. And, of course, the more objective you are, the less likely you are to let your emotions get the better of you and the more successful your negotiations will be.

Finally, having that accurate data makes you better able to prepare value-creating offers that are likely to meet with positive responses from your customers. Remember, it's ultimately trading those items that are valued more than they cost that enables you to create true business value. And the only way to get all those items on the table and trade them is by validating both sides' CNA and Wish List Estimations. It's these steps that enable you to go beyond a simple "win-win" solution and help you establish a solid, mutually beneficial, long-term relationship with your customers.

Just in case you have any doubts whether this works, here's an example of how it worked for me. Many years ago I fell in love with a classic 1955 steel gray Chevy pickup truck that I saw parked on the side of the road with a "For Sale" sign on the windshield. The asking price was $13,500. Using the Strategic Negotiation Process to blueprint the negotiation, the first thing I did was estimate the CNA for my side. The two possibilities were that I would either buy a different truck or no truck at all, but I knew the most likely CNA was the first. Even so, when I analyzed the effects of that CNA, I realized that as much as I wanted to buy this particular truck, there were several others I could buy, most of which were priced at less than $13,500. At the same time, buying one of the others would have required me to travel out of state, which carried some risk itself. I might, for example, make the trip and then discover when I saw the truck that I didn't like it, in which case I'd have to drive home without it, having wasted a lot of time and effort in the process.

Having done the CNA Estimation for my side, I then did the analysis for the seller. Although I knew that his CNA would be either to sell the truck to someone else or to keep it, it seemed more likely to me that he would sell it to someone else. So my next step was to determine the effects of that CNA on the seller. Basically, what I needed to know was what "someone else" would most likely be willing to pay for the truck. There were two ways to get this data: talking to others and doing a search of public records.

I began with the search, going to an online seller of automobiles, where I learned that about 300 1955 Chevy pickups were available for sale around the United States and that the average selling price for a completely rebuilt, "showroom quality" truck was $11,500. Then I went to talk to the automobile consignment shop that was selling this truck for its owner. (The owner, incidentally, was one of the cast members of the popular television show *Taxi*, who was selling an entire antique car collection—and was trying to do it quickly). My purpose in speaking to the broker was to get a sense of how both the seller and the broker saw or perceived their CNA.

While I was speaking to the broker and asking questions to validate my estimation, I learned two key pieces of information that would help me formulate an offer. The first was that the current owner had overpaid considerably for the truck—he'd bought it just a year earlier for $17,500. The second key piece of information was that he had turned down several offers for $12,500. Can you imagine: this same truck was trading for $11,500 nationally, they'd had offers that were $1,000 higher, and they'd turned them down! Why? Because they had misdiagnosed their CNA based on their earlier bad decision; that is, they thought—incorrectly— that they'd be able to sell the car to someone else for their asking price of $13,500. (You'll remember that earlier we said that you should accept an offer as long as it's better than your CNA. But this can be a problem when either you've not diagnosed your CNA at all or you've misdiagnosed it, as happened in this case.)

At this point I had both estimated the seller's CNA and validated it through my Web search and my conversation with the broker. My goal was to buy the truck at its market value, which was $11,500. I knew, though, that having paid significantly more for the truck, the current owner was unlikely to be happy about selling it to me at that price. Nevertheless, as I've already mentioned, one of the benefits of doing the estimation and validation is that gathering accurate data—not perfect, but at least directionally accurate, data—can diffuse a potentially emotional situation like this one.

Given what I knew about the owner, I wasn't at all surprised when the broker asked me if I was crazy when I finally made an offer of $11,500 for the truck, as he had already turned down an offer of $12,500. But when I showed him the printout from the Web showing what the same truck was selling for elsewhere, he had to agree that it was a fair price. Eventually, the owner did accept my offer, although only after the broker showed him the printout. After the negotiation, the broker told me that the information I'd provided was the key to making the deal.

The point of all this is that estimating the CNA and validating it, especially in a single-issue, zero-sum negotiation like this one, can make all the difference. Here was what appeared to be an almost impossible situation. The owner had made a bad decision to overpay for the truck, another potential buyer had made a bad decision by offering more than the truck's market value, and, as a result, the owner had misdiagnosed his Consequences of No Agreement. But by my finding hard data and using it to educate the owner about his real CNA, the seller got a fair price for his truck and I got a fair deal on a classic.

Here's what this deal looks like in terms of the Agreement Zone. As you can see, based on another buyer's offer of $12,500 and the owner's asking price of $13,500, the owner thought the Agreement Zone was somewhere between those two figures, so my offer of $11,500 wasn't even in the zone. But by diagnosing the zone, finding out what the owner thought it was, and using the data to adjust his thinking, I was able to make the deal.

Seller's Irrational Agreement Zone Based on Misdiagnosed CNA

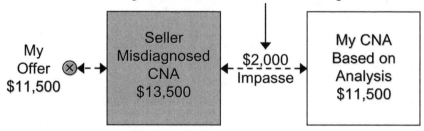

| My Offer $11,500 | Seller Misdiagnosed CNA $13,500 | $2,000 Impasse | My CNA Based on Analysis $11,500 |

To be honest, this process doesn't always work in the end because you can't always count on the other side's reacting well to this kind of rational data analysis. However, the process is designed to increase the odds that deals work well and in your favor, and it does help more often than not—and certainly more often than the reactive approach that most people use.

Before I go on to show you how this step works, there's one other point you should bear in mind. Although you will have already determined in the previous step what information you're guessing at and what you don't know, it's advisable to review all that information before you go on to validate it. This time, though, be really hard on yourself. We are typically rewarded for showing others how well we know something, but at this stage you should be rewarded for "blowing holes" in your own earlier estimations. The harder you are on yourself, the better data you'll have and the higher the probability that you'll do well in the face-to-face phases of the negotiation. Again, the other side probably won't spend much time analyzing what it doesn't know, much less analyzing the deal from your perspective; but if used properly, this can be to your advantage.

To reiterate, the validation step essentially consists of three parts, the first of which is validating the CNA and Wish List Estimations by gathering information from others in your organization and from public sources. To make it as easy as possible to understand how this step works, I'm going to discuss the CNA Validation first and then the Wish List Validation.

VALIDATING THE CONSEQUENCES OF NO AGREEMENT ESTIMATION

In the first step of the Strategic Negotiation Process, covered in Chapter 4, you estimated both your own CNA and your customer's, with the understanding that you would still need additional information about the latter. This second step is designed to enable you to determine whether your initial estimation was correct and to fill in whatever blanks there may be.

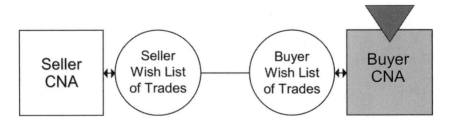

Some of the things people are typically still unsure of after their initial estimation are:

- What really is the other side's CNA?
- What are the elements of that CNA?
- Are those elements costs or benefits, hard or soft, and short term or long term?
- How does the other side see its CNA?

In the initial estimation of the other side's CNA, you used what you knew about the customer from prior dealings with him or her, your understanding of the customer's needs from the sales process, and your personal knowledge of both your most likely competitor and other alternatives that the buyer might have. But now it's time to broaden your knowledge of the other side's CNA by looking for answers beyond yourself to others in your organization.

Gathering Information from Others in Your Organization

The most likely sources of information in your organization are those who have handled this customer before, those who have worked for the customer, and those who have worked for your most likely competitor in this deal. Virtually every organization I've ever been in employs people who have worked for either its customers or its competitors. I have found, though, that the hardest thing to do is to find out exactly who those people are. In addition, the larger the selling organization, the harder it is to find them. At the same time, however, the larger the selling organization, the more likely it is that people are there who will be able to help you.

The most effective way to find these people is to reach out to as many department heads as possible. These should, of course, include those within the sales function, but it should also include people in manufacturing, finance, marketing, and other departments. Let those department heads know you are involved in a very important negotiation with the customer, ask them if anyone in their group has worked for or with the customer or for one of your competitors, and tell them that you would appreciate those individuals providing you with 10 to 15 minutes of coaching. Once you've reached someone who can help, you should ask that individual to provide you with as much information as he or she can covering the four questions noted above.

Of course, exactly from whom you choose to solicit information depends on what you've estimated the other side's CNA in this negotiation to be. For example, one of our clients is a provider of data and data services, so of the three most common customer CNAs—buying from one of their competitors, doing it themselves, or doing nothing (i.e., spending the money on something else)—our client's salespeople often found themselves up against the second. "Why should we buy from you?" they heard from potential customers. "We can build it ourselves, and it'll not only be cheaper but it'll be better customized for our needs."

Faced with this situation, the company's salespeople went to those in their organization who had the responsibility for designing, implementing, and managing databases. What they asked the designers for was a sense of the elements of the client's choice to build their own database, things like collecting the data, rationalizing the data, updating the data, global versus national data, maintaining accuracy, and so on. Armed with that knowledge, the salespeople were better able to formulate specific questions about each element of the customer's CNA and determine, for each of those elements, whether it would actually be better for the customer to do it themselves.

Researching Publicly Available Data

Although the best sources of data are typically yourself, those within your organization, and your customer, there's also a wealth of publicly available information that can be very useful to you in validating your estimations of the customer's CNA. Bear in mind that in the validation step you want to gather all the relevant and accurate data you can so whether someone says "I can get it better, cheaper, and faster elsewhere," "I can build my own," or "I can use the money better for something else," you'll be able to dissect those statements and consider every element that should be considered. And there's a wide variety of publicly available data that can help you do that, including industry journals, industry trade associations, independent third-party analyses (such as white papers), and Lexis/Nexus searches. Sometimes, in fact, sources like these can present you with real finds.

For example, one of our clients is a firm that sells vitamin supplements to local and factory farms that produce chicken, beef, and pork. The supplements can be delivered to the animals in several different forms, the two main ones being powder and liquid. Some of the firm's clients argue that one or the other form is better, faster, and cheaper; and some argue that the efficacy and ease of use for the other is greater. But the fact is that neither form is *always* better—it depends on a variety of other factors. Using publicly available data, such as industry white papers, articles, and studies comparing the two primary methods, our client's salespeople can determine which is most advantageous in any given situation. They can then use the facts to counter irrational arguments and old-school tactics, and adjust the customer's thinking to a more reality-based CNA. Again, it's important to remember here that the customer sees your offer as a gain or loss based on his or her perception of the CNA, so it's essential that you make sure that perception is accurate.

VALIDATING THE WISH LIST ESTIMATION

When I discussed the Wish List Estimation in Chapter 5, I talked about the items that are most likely to be important to your customers in any deal—length of contract, volume, price, payment terms, and service—and showed how you could estimate what the other side might want in each of these areas. But those estimates were essentially just educated guesses, so now it's time to find out exactly how good those guesses were. It's important to bear in mind here that although the process for validating the Consequences of No Agreement and Wish List Estimations are similar, they are not identical.

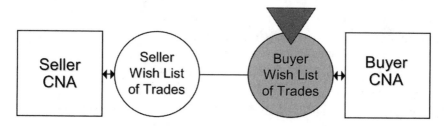

As with the CNA, the validation of your Wish List Estimation requires you to remember there's no such thing as a generic negotiation and that you must accordingly look at each negotiation specifically in terms of the product or service being sold, who the competitors are, and who the customer is. However, unlike the CNA, for which you can get information from both public sources and other people, validating the Wish List Estimation is accomplished entirely through the latter. There are, not surprisingly, very few public sources, either in print or on the Internet, that can provide you with information on what the other side wants in any given negotiation. But you can get that information both by asking questions of people within your organization and by asking your customer directly.

Regardless of the source of this information, validating the Wish List Estimation essentially means getting good answers to three questions:

- Are these the right items?
- What is most to least important?
- How important are the top few items?

Gathering Information from Others in Your Organization

I suggested earlier that when you're validating your customer's CNA, you should look not just for salespeople but for people throughout your organization who have worked for or with your customer or for one of your competitors. This is because the CNA and its elements can encompass so many aspects of your customer's business that you need to be able to call on people who know about all those aspects. Validating the Wish List Estimation, however, is, at least in a sense, less complicated, if no less important.

As already noted, both sellers and buyers in the vast majority of negotiations are primarily interested in a handful of items, including price, payment terms, service, length of contract, and volume. For that reason, to validate your customer's Wish List Estimation, it is of primary importance that you contact people within your organization who have been specifically involved in sales—selling to your customer, buying for your customer, or selling for your most likely competitor in this deal. Once you've determined who these people are, the most effective way of gaining information from them is to show them the Wish List Estimation you've developed and ask them, based on their knowledge and experience, the answers to the three questions noted above.

B e s t   P r a c t i c e s   R e v i e w

- Find and consult with those in your organization who have worked with your customer, for your customer, and/or for your competitor on this deal. Their help will be invaluable in validating both the CNA and Wish List Estimations.
- Do searches of publicly available data to validate your customer's CNA, including industry publications, white papers, and industry associations.

C o m m o n   M i s t a k e s   t o   A v o i d

- Looking for publicly available data on your customer's Wish List. It's rarely ever available.
- Getting stuck in the trap of using validation to reinforce what you want to believe. It's important that you focus on the real facts of this negotiation, even if you don't particularly like or agree with them.

· · · · ·

Thus far you have developed a goal to "create joint value and divide it given concerns for fairness in the ongoing relationship," conducted Consequences of No Agreement and Wish List Estimations for both sides in the negotiation, and begun to validate your estimations by soliciting help from others in your organization and from public sources. Although both are excellent sources of information about your customer, the ultimate source is always the customers themselves. And the best way to get information from them is to ask for it. But there are many ways of soliciting information, and depending on how you do it, you will find yourself with anything from no useful information at all to an enormous amount of data that you can apply to the negotiation. The next part of the validation step, preparing for the validation meeting with your customer, is designed to enable you to elicit as much good information as possible and to do so in a way that will not only not alienate your customer but, in fact, make him or her eager to continue working with you. And that part of the step is the subject of the next chapter.

7

STEP TWO
VALIDATING THE
ESTIMATION

PART TWO
Preparing for the Validation Meeting

Now that you've started validating the Consequences of No Agreement and Wish List Estimations by gathering information from others in your organization and from public sources, it's time to go to the second part of the validation step: preparing for the validation meeting with your customer.

Estimate	Validate	Create Value	Divide Value
⊕ CNA	⊕ In-House/Public Sources	⊕ Exceed CNAs	⊕ Anchor on MEO
⊕ Wish List of Trades	⊕ **Meeting Preparation**	⊕ Look for Trades	⊕ Trading
	⊕ Validation Meeting		⊕ Claim Value

Again, in blueprinting a negotiation your customer is ultimately the best source of information about what he or she needs and wants from the negotiation. However, because validating CNA and Wish Lists have different requirements, they also require different approaches. And because of that, it is essential that you prepare in advance for the validation meeting with your customer. As I did in the last chapter, I begin here with the CNA and then go on to the Wish List Validation.

VALIDATING THE CONSEQUENCES OF NO AGREEMENT ESTIMATION

Although information from your customers about their CNA can be, quite literally, invaluable, getting that information out of them isn't necessarily easy, primarily for two reasons. The first is that even though people are generally more than happy to tell you what they want out of a deal with you—their Wish List—they're much less likely to tell you what would happen to them if they don't make the deal with you. The other reason is that, as noted before, the chances are they haven't even thought about what would happen to them if you don't reach an agreement, or they have thought about it but have misdiagnosed it. In either case, even if they wanted to tell you their CNA or its positive and negative effects, they wouldn't be able to.

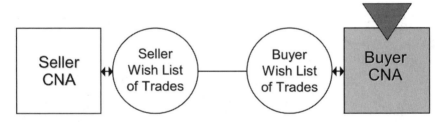

Despite this inherent difficulty, you have the advantage of having already learned a great deal about your customer through the estimation step and the first part of the validation step; and you can build on that information to develop questions that will provide you with the kind of information you're looking for. It's important to note, however, that the questions and answers won't provide only a learning experience for you but for your customer as well, so that ultimately you'll both benefit from the exchange. Even if they don't answer your questions, this step provides you with an opportunity to educate them about your knowledge of their CNA.

Preparing Questions for Your Customers

Because of all the information you've already gathered in the Strategic Negotiation Process, preparing CNA-related questions for the other side is actually quite simple. First, you review a customer's most likely CNA and all the elements you've already estimated. Then you formulate an obvious question for each—a simple question about what would happen to your customer if they don't make a deal with you. Finally, because you're not likely to get a simple answer to a simple question, as I mentioned, you restate each question in three "less obvious" ways.

Getting all the elements of their CNA on the table. As you well know, customers generally oversimplify the negotiation (e.g., "Your competition is cheaper") and overestimate the positive aspects of their own CNA (e.g., "They're also better and faster"). For that reason, once you've determined your customer's CNA, it's essential that you get all of the various positive and negative elements of that CNA out on the table so they can be taken into consideration in a total value proposition–to–value proposition comparison.

Let's say, for example, that you're involved in a negotiation in which the other side has told you that one of your competitors is better, faster, and cheaper than you, or maybe just cheaper, and that they will go with the competitor if you can't come to an agreement. Now that you know their CNA, what you have to do is look at all of the elements of that CNA, not just price but also such things as service, product quality, design, delivery, installation, impact on the customer's customer, financial and/or political risk, ease of use, and ability of your competitor to grow long term with the customer. In other words, you must have a clear idea of all of the decision criteria your customer "should" be using when they compare the value proposition of your firm against your competitor's.

What you're doing in this exercise, then, is focusing on what the consequences will be for your customer if they don't reach agreement with you, what they will choose and how that will affect them, and whether that choice is actually better than choosing you. The key is to put yourself in their shoes and think through, from every stakeholder involved on their side, all of the various effects of not making a deal with you, decide whether those elements represent a plus or a minus for them, and then prepare questions that both educate them on their CNA and provide you a perspective about how they see it.

Preparing questions for each element. Once you feel that you've clearly thought through the other side's CNA as well as all of its elements, the next step is to prepare the "obvious" question for each of them. The questions shouldn't be difficult to prepare as they represent the most important things you need to know to validate your customer's CNA. Let's use, as examples, some of the areas I considered in the Estimation Step— design, delivery, and installation. If your potential customer is considering going to one of your competitors, this is one of the obvious questions you'd want to ask: "How easy and effective is the competitor's design process compared with ours?" Similarly, you would like to be able to ask the other side: "How accurate, timely, and efficient is the competitor's delivery process compared with ours?" And, finally, in regard to installation, you need an answer to this question: "How easy and safe is the competitor's installation process, and how much work disruption would changing suppliers cause in your organization?"

These are good, straightforward questions, and if the people on the other side would give you good, straightforward answers, you'd have all the information you needed. Unfortunately, however, that's not likely to happen. In fact, for the reasons I noted above, the likelihood of getting a direct answer to any of these questions is, at best, slim. But you still need the information, so you have to find another way of getting it. Restating the questions in less obvious ways is a good way to do that.

Restating each question in three less obvious ways. Restating an obvious question about an element of your customer's CNA in a less obvious way is somewhat—but not much more—difficult than stating an obvious one. The best way to do this is to break down the question into its component parts. That is, rather than raising a general question, think of more specific aspects of the question and ask about those.

Let's take the first obvious question as an example: "How easy and effective is the competitor's design process compared with ours?" Three different—and less obvious—ways to state that question might be the following:

- "What percentage of our competitor's solution is customized, and how do they charge for it?"

- "How many man-hours would be required by your organization to complete the design process with our competitor?"
- "What is the timeline for our competitor's design process?"

If you were to ask these questions, you would essentially get some of the answers you need about your competitor's design process when compared with yours. But there's an even better way of doing it. Keep in mind that you should have already estimated the answers to these questions during the estimation step. By embedding your estimations into the questions, you can make the questions even more effective in two ways. First, it shows the people on the other side that you know the facts, that you've done your homework. And at the same time it educates them about the facts in the event that they haven't properly thought through all of the elements of their own CNA. This is actually a customer benefit in that it provides customers with the facts they must have to make the best decision given their needs.

For example, if you have a sense that you have superiority over your competitor in this area, by embedding data into your questions, you can get the people on the other side to confirm or deny it by asking these questions:

- "As you know, virtually 85 percent of our solution is customized and included in the purchase price. What sort of customization does the competitor do? I understand they have a 10 percent price premium for customization."
- "Our company guarantees the maximum hours that your organization has to invest in customization. How do other firms handle that?"
- "Most of the industry has targeted installation timelines with no project scope changes. Our firm has guaranteed installation timelines with limited project scope changes. How does this factor into your analysis of our company versus our competitor?"

The benefit of asking these "less obvious" questions is that, generally speaking, the more direct the question, the less likely you'll get a useful answer. On the other hand, even though asking a more general question is likely to elicit a more honest and "safe" answer, the chances are that the information you'll receive will be less relevant for your purposes.

This is one of the reasons I suggest you ask two or three questions for each element of the other side's CNA. Multiple answers to a series of questions are much more likely to yield good data than the answer to any one question.

You'll notice that in these examples I've used the terms *our competitor* or *the industry* rather than naming a particular organization. I do that because I've found that asking about a specific competitor frequently yields a more conservative answer from the other side. I also have to admit, however, that while asking a question about the industry generally elicits responses that are more open, it also allows you less opportunity to show the other side how much you know about the competitor's value proposition (the customer's CNA) for this deal.

To give you a better idea of how all of this works, let's look again at the data and data services provider I used as an example earlier. You'll remember that when faced with a client's CNA of "We can build our own database, and it'll be cheaper and more customized than if we buy from you," the salespeople went to those in their own organization responsible for designing, implementing, and managing databases. They asked them to provide a sense of the elements of the client's choice to build their own database, things like collecting data, rationalizing it, updating it, and the like. The salespeople then looked at each of these elements in an effort to determine if it would actually be better for the customer to build their own database. Finally, with the help of the database designers, the salespeople were able to develop a series of questions to ask the customer in order to validate their estimations in five different areas.

Design Elements Questions

- "Who in your organization has the skill to design a database?"
- "Who will handle their job function while they are building it?"
- "How long do you anticipate it will take?"
- "What steps are involved in the design process?"
- "How will global versus national data be collected?"

Implementation Elements Questions

- "How difficult do you think it would be to integrate this database with your existing systems?"
- "How long do you think it will take? How long before beta testing?"

Risk Elements Questions

- "What happens if the head of your design group changes jobs in the middle of the project?"
- "What will the internal consequences be if an internally designed system fails? (Of course, if we do it and it fails, it's our fault.)"
- "How will you handle budget overruns? (If we do it, the cost is guaranteed.)"

Outcome and Ongoing Maintenance Questions

- "How will custom reports be built and charged for?"
- "How will updates and data accuracy be maintained?"
- "How will service be handled on evenings and weekends? (As you know, we provide 24/7 service globally.)"

No doubt you've gotten the point by now. As you can see, with questions like these, even if the other side doesn't give you open and honest answers, you will still get a good sense of how they see their CNA. And if they haven't properly diagnosed their CNA, you'll actually be helping them by creating some FUD (fear, uncertainty, and doubt) about it.

As in anything, there are, of course, potential pitfalls in this process. The first of these is being overly confident about the quality of your initial estimation. If you are and as a result feel little need to add more validation, you may well find yourself with a lot of inaccurate and, ultimately, useless information. At the same time, there is also a risk of asking a great number of nonrelevant questions and leaving the validation meeting with lots of data but little information that is useful in validating your estimations. A third potential problem is asking questions that are either too direct and not getting good answers or too vague and getting equally poor responses.

It's only by preparing, asking, and getting answers to multiple, well-thought-out questions that you'll be able to see a pattern by which you can learn how the other side perceives its CNA, as well as how to diplomatically educate them about what they don't know. Remember, the single most important reason for proper CNA estimation and validation is that the other side sees your offer as a gain or loss depending on their perception of their CNA. So before you even think about making an offer, it's essential that you know more about their CNA than they do, that you understand how they see their CNA, and that you adjust their thinking through good question preparation and delivery. Then, and only then, should you make an offer.

Validating the Other Side's Consequences of No Agreement Estimation

Now that you have an idea of how to validate the other side's CNA, it's time for you to apply that knowledge to your own negotiating situation. Go back to the data you recorded in Chapter 4 under "Consequences of No Agreement—The Other Side" and review your customer's CNA as well as the short-term and long-term hard and soft costs and benefits associated with that CNA.

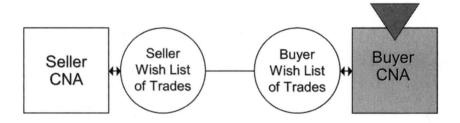

As mentioned before, this is a good time to take another hard look at that information to make sure that you are fully satisfied that it's reasonably accurate given what you learned by talking to others in your organization and using publicly available data. Now, applying the concepts I've discussed in this chapter, for each element of your customer's CNA, develop an "obvious" question about that element in the space on page 103 and then two or three "less obvious" questions.

• • • • •

Now that you have completed the preparation for the CNA-related aspect of the validation meeting with your customer, it's time to prepare for the Wish List–related aspect.

**CONSEQUENCES OF NO AGREEMENT VALIDATION QUESTIONS—
THE OTHER SIDE**

Customer's CNA: _____

Element 1: _____

Obvious Question: _____

Restatement A: _____

Restatement B: _____

Restatement C: _____

Element 2: _____

Obvious Question: _____

Restatement A: _____

Restatement B: _____

Restatement C: _____

Element 3: _____

Obvious Question: _____

Restatement A: _____

Restatement B: _____

Restatement C: _____

Element 4: _____

Obvious Question: _____

Restatement A: _____

Restatement B: _____

Restatement C: _____

VALIDATING THE WISH LIST ESTIMATION

Interestingly, getting information from your customers to validate your Wish List Estimation is considerably easier than doing so for your CNA Estimation, and for one simple reason. While your customer is, understandably, not likely to be too comfortable talking about what might happen to them if they don't make a deal with you—assuming, of course, that they've even given it any thought—they're usually more— even if not completely—comfortable in saying, "These are the items that I want in the final deal." As one of our purchasing clients says, "How will you get what you want if you don't ask for it!"

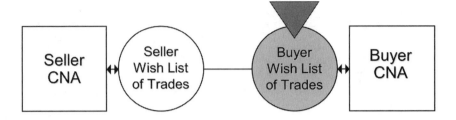

Preparing Questions for Your Customer

As noted in the last chapter, validating your customer's Wish List Estimation essentially means getting good answers to three questions:

1. Are these the right items?
2. What is most to least important?
3. How important are the top few items?

Again, however, there are numerous ways to solicit information, and the more obvious you are, the less likely it is that you'll get the information you're looking for. Even if customers are more likely to answer questions about their Wish List, it's still advantageous for you to soften the questions a bit. What you have to do, then, is look at the list of items your customer is most likely to be concerned about, rephrase the three questions above, and, as necessary, ask follow-up questions. Here's the list again, as well as some examples of different ways to ask the questions:

Typical Buyer Wish List Estimation			
Rank	*Item*	*Weight*	*Range (High to Low)*
1.	Price	40%	$14–$18
2.	Payment terms	20%	60–45 days
3.	Service	20%	24/7 – 12/7
4.	Length of contract	10%	0–2 years
5.	Volume	10%	1–2,000 units

Typical buyer Wish List Estimation validation questions. To answer the question: "Are these the right items?"

- "I understand that in the upcoming negotiation you would like to talk about price, volume, length of contract, service, and volume. Is that right?"
- "Is there anything missing?"
- "Is there anything here that shouldn't be?"

To answer the question: "What is most to least important?"

- "OK, now that I have a clearer list, can you help me to organize it in terms of items most to least important to you?"
- "I understand that they're all important, but if you had to rank them highest to lowest on your priority list, how would you do that?"

To answer the question: "How important are the top few items?"

- "Now that I see that price, length of contract, and service are the most important issues to you, how important is each?
- "If you had to weight the top three, how heavily would each be weighted? I mean, would price be 50 percent and the others 25 percent each, or would it be some other combination?"

Generally speaking, getting the answers to these questions enables you to determine how accurate your initial estimates were and, if necessary, adjust those estimates to reflect what you've learned. More specifically, the first question makes it possible for you to make sure that you and your customer are on the same page in terms of what items the customer is primarily concerned with. The second and third questions get those on the other side to recognize that some items are more important than others and, accordingly, which are critical and which might be traded away. Remember, trades come from the two sides valuing several items differently.

Here's an example of how this works in practice. I was consulting with a client in Chicago—a consumer advertising agency—that was negotiating the purchase of an equity share in some Internet-based human resource technology from a professor and his wife from the Midwest. The professor and his wife had developed the technology themselves and at the outset told the agency that they were interested in discussing only one item: how much the agency was willing to pay them for a share of the technology. That they were acting as if the technology were a commodity was bad enough. But to make matters worse, like most of us who have developed something ourselves, the professor and his wife were overvaluing the technology by a considerable amount.

Sitting down in a planning meeting with the agency, we began by reviewing our goal to "create joint value and divide it given concerns for fairness in the ongoing relationship." We then conducted CNA and Wish List Estimations for both ourselves and for the professor and his wife. It was very clear, though, that before we could even get to the issues of ranking, weighting, and the rest, the first thing we had to do was to get them to think beyond merely price. To do that, based on our estimations, we prepared a long list of questions for them.

But we also had to find a way to *ask* the professor and his wife our questions, so we suggested getting together for what we called a "prenegotiation" meeting to work through some fact-finding and joint investigation. We—the ad agency and Think!—clearly defined this as an official part of validating the blueprint, which is something very few people do. It worked to our advantage, though, because it allowed the other side to feel freer and more conversational. So even though they insisted, "There's not much to talk about—either you pay our price or you don't," they agreed to the chat.

When we did get together, these were some of the questions we asked:

- "Other than price, what else will be negotiated at the final settlement?"
- "How about equity?"
- "How will we handle cash flow? How will it be distributed?"
- "What about subsequent releases of technology?"
- "How will we handle consulting projects that come out of this technology?"
- "How will we handle training projects that come out of this technology?"
- "Who will carry the insurance?"
- "Whose server will the technology sit on? Who will handle service?"

By asking these questions and others like it, we were able to start the professor and his wife thinking about items other than price. At the

same time, we asked some well-thought-out questions about their consequences of not reaching agreement with us, and we released some strategic information about our consequences of not reaching agreement
with them. By the time the meeting was over, we had gone a long way toward broadening the negotiation and redistributing power. In fact, we
all felt good about this prenegotiation meeting, which, as it turned out,
was actually the most strategic aspect of the negotiation—as it typically
is—and benefited both sides.

As with learning any new process, there are of course pitfalls that
you should try to avoid. One of the most common pitfalls in preparing
Wish List validation questions is overcomplicating them. If the questions
are too complicated, you get overcomplicated answers that yield little
useful data. Alternatively, if you ask questions that are too broad, you
wind up with too much general data. Ideally, you should ask simple, but
specific, questions, as these are the ones that are most likely to elicit the
data you really need. Remember that ultimately what you want to know
is what they want, what is most to least important to them, and how important the top few items are.

Validating the Other Side's Wish List Estimation

Now that you have a better idea of how to validate the Wish List Estimation, it's time for you to apply the process by preparing some questions for your own negotiation. Go back to the Wish List Estimation in
Chapter 5, in which you estimated those items you thought the other
side would want included in the final deal.

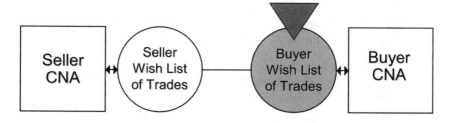

Now, taking into account the information and advice you received
from talking to your colleagues, review the estimates carefully, and hon-
estly challenge yourself on what could still be improved. Then, use the

---

WISH LIST ESTIMATION

The Other Side

Rank	Item	Weight	Range (High to Low)
1.	_____	_____	_____
2.	_____	_____	_____
3.	_____	_____	_____
4.	_____	_____	_____
5.	_____	_____	_____
6.	_____	_____	_____
7.	_____	_____	_____
8.	_____	_____	_____

---

outline below to develop a list of questions to validate your estimation of the other side's Wish List.

Wish List Validation questions—the other side.

To answer the question: "Are these the right items?"

- "I understand that in the upcoming negotiation you would like to talk about _____. _____, _____, _____, _____, and _____. Is that right?"
- "Is there anything missing"
- "Is there anything here that shouldn't be?"

To answer the question: "What is most to least important?"

- "OK, now that I have a clearer list, can you help me to organize the items in terms of most to least important to you?"
- "I understand that they're all important, but if you had to rank them highest to lowest on your priority list, how would you do that?"

To answer the question: "How important are the top few items?"

- "Now that I see that _____, _____, and _____ are the most important issues to you, how important is each?

- "If you had to weight the top three, how heavily would each be weighted? I mean, would price be 50 percent and the others 25 percent each, or would it be some other combination?"

DEALING WITH Professional Buyers

You'll recall that in earlier discussions of professional buyers I pointed out that such buyers normally work on behalf of internal customers and that those customers are satisfied not by sourcing the cheapest product available but by having all their needs met. So when you're preparing questions to validate your Consequences of No Agreement, you should take these stakeholders into account and think about what their needs are and how this purchase will affect them. Ask the buyer about their CNA—not only about your competitor's price but about value-added support, upgrades, global access, and other issues.

Similarly, when you're preparing questions to validate your Wish List Estimations, you should think not only about price but about all the various items on the customer's Wish List. As already noted, it's best if you can get access to the buyer's internal customers. But—particularly if you haven't been able to—showing that you've taken the time to analyze their CNA and Wish Lists by embedding information into your validation questions enables you to subtly anchor professional buyers to a more thorough CNA analysis as well as to all the elements of their Wish List.

Best Practices Review

- Always embed details of your estimation into your validation questions. That way, even if the other side doesn't answer them, at least you'll have shared some facts with them and perhaps crated some FUD.

Common Mistakes to Avoid

- Preparing CNA questions that are too direct, such as "What do you see as my competitor's main weakness?" Rather, soften the questions by asking them in two or three less direct ways.

Thus far you have developed a goal to "create joint value and divide it given concern for fairness in the ongoing relationship," conducted Consequences of No Agreement and Wish List Estimations for both sides in the negotiation, and started to validate or improve your estimates by using public sources, asking questions of colleagues, and preparing to solicit information in a meeting with your customer. That meeting, which is the last part of the validation step, is covered in the next chapter.

8

STEP TWO
VALIDATING THE
ESTIMATION

PART THREE
Conducting the Validation Meeting

Now that you've completed the first two parts of the validation step—gathering information from colleagues and public sources and preparing for the validation meeting with your customer—it's time to go to the final part, the meeting itself.

Estimate	Validate	Create Value	Divide Value
⊕ CNA	⊕ In-House/Public Sources	⊕ Exceed CNAs	⊕ Anchor on MEO
⊕ Wish List of Trades	⊕ Meeting Preparation	⊕ Look for Trades	⊕ Trading
	⊕ **Validation Meeting**		⊕ Claim Value

Of course, few sellers or buyers think of this face-to-face validation of their estimations as part of the negotiation. They see it, if they consider it at all, as "planning" for the negotiation. In fact, this phase of the Strategic Negotiation Process is not only part of the negotiation but is one of the most—if not *the* most—critical and central aspects. It's in this phase of the negotiation—the validation meeting—that you will be able to do the following:

- Educate your customer about their CNA
- Educate your customer about your CNA
- Learn more about the items on your customer's Wish List
- Help your customer rank and weight the items on their Wish List
- Share the items on your Wish List with your customer
- Broaden the trading beyond single-item, zero-sum concessions

Notwithstanding these potential results, in a sense only two things are really going on in a validation meeting. The first of these is *sharing and trading information.* Paradoxically, the fact that most customers don't even see sharing information as part of the negotiation actually works to your benefit because, as a result, they're likely to share more freely. Ultimately, of course, it's trading information that enables you to learn more about what your customer wants and to let him or her know better what you want. And that, in turn, is what enables you to formulate offers that, by trading as many items as possible, exceed both sides' CNA and create real value. Later on in this chapter I'll tell you about some of the tactics you can use to facilitate sharing information.

The second thing that's going on in a validation meeting is one side or the other—or both—*using that sharing and trading of information to set the tone for the negotiation.* This is done by establishing what G. B. Northcraft and M. A. Neale call an "anchor" in their article, "Amateurs, Experts and Real Estate: An Anchoring and Adjustment Perspective on Property Pricing Decisions" (*Organizational Behavior and Human Decision Process,* 39, 1987). An anchor is a starting point for one aspect of a negotiation or, in some instances, an entire negotiation. An anchor can be true or false, appropriate or inappropriate, in any given negotiation. Nevertheless, only anchors that are both true and appropriate can be beneficial to both you and your customer, as only such anchors will enable you to create value.

ANCHORING

In sales negotiations, there are two types of anchors—opening offers and other items—both of which can have an enormous impact on the outcome of a negotiation. On a very basic level, opening offers can be defined as the first offer put on the table by either party. It could be your saying, "We always sell our Gizmos for $15 per unit," or your customer's saying, "We never pay more than $12 per unit for Gizmos." In reality, though, it's not quite that simple. For example, if a customer sends out a request for a proposal (RFP) and asks you to respond in a certain way, they have, in a sense at least, made an opening offer and anchored the negotiation. Regardless of the form the offer takes, however, the most important thing to bear in mind is that opening offers have a greater effect on outcomes than all of the subsequent trades combined. In the next two chapters I provide a great deal of information on preparing and presenting what we consider to be the ultimate opening offers.

Nonopening-offer anchors, which I discuss in this chapter, can be just as important, and both sellers and buyers use a wide range of such anchors—either intentionally or otherwise—in negotiations. Nonopening-offer anchors almost invariably concern individual items rather than multiple ones and range anywhere from a customer deciding, arbitrarily, that they want a 12 percent discount in price this year to a customer insisting that they won't pay more than they did ten years ago for a product whose price has since doubled. Although some nonopening-offer anchors are appropriate, the vast majority are either untrue or inappropriate, if not simply irrational. Some other examples include:

- Customers who anchor on the statement "I can get the same thing cheaper elsewhere." This may or may not be true, but buyers use this argument for one very good reason—it works. In this case, it tends to anchor the negotiation on "I need to get a better price to beat the competition" rather than "I need to sell more value."
- Customers who anchor the negotiation by saying that a particular price is "beyond their budget." This may be true, but it's actually an inappropriate anchor because, in fact, the customer's budget has nothing to do with the price you set for your products or services—or, at least, it shouldn't. Even so, it works as an anchor and, more often than not, to your detriment.
- Reps who give huge discounts in the fourth quarter or push overly hard on price and then move on, leaving their replacements with a customer who is already anchored on past negotiation behaviors. Although this is also an inappropriate anchor, such behaviors

in these situations influence both the tone and direction of the replacements' first negotiation with the customer.

- Salesforces that publish price lists. Although this serves as a way of communicating pricing to customers, it's also inappropriate as an anchor for those firms that wish to sell value propositions or solutions, because reps still tend to be surprised when, as a result, a customer wants to anchor on price at the same time the rep is trying to anchor on value.

But such anchors are by no means limited to price—they can come from a wide variety of sources. One of the many ways that a negotiation can be intentionally or unwittingly anchored is through the sales process. For example, if in the sales process you've done a great job of anchoring on selling the total value of your company's solution to the customer, in all likelihood that's the kind of package you'll end up negotiating. On the other hand, if in the sales process you've only called on the lowest-level purchasing agent, and she's been pushing hard for you to offer them the lowest price, price is most likely what you'll end up negotiating. The old adage "You negotiate what you sell" is true. The quality of the sales process does have an impact on how easy or difficult the negotiation is.

You and your customer can also become anchored, intentionally or otherwise, on a particular way of negotiating, which can have an impact on future negotiations. For example, we once worked with a buying organization that loved to use the old school tactic of "nibbling," coming back after the negotiation had apparently ended to ask for a little bit more. They loved this tactic and for a very good reason—it always seemed to work for them. But when I asked them to think about it from the suppliers' perspective and how the suppliers reacted to it, they realized that what they'd actually been doing was teaching their suppliers to lie to them. Because the suppliers had learned over time to expect the buyer to use this tactic, they would always hold something back. Then, when the buyer began nibbling, the suppliers would appear to be giving the buyer something more, even though they really weren't. If you've been anchored in a situation like that, it can easily take multiple negotiations to enable you and your customer to reanchor on trust, share information, trade, and ultimately create value.

The Effects of Anchoring

Although it's probably easy for you to see how anchors like those described can have an impact on a negotiation, here's an example of exactly how it happens. Think! runs Strategic Negotiation Process workshops in companies all around the world, part of which include practice negotiations based on real-life conditions in those companies' industries. What we do, essentially, is take all the people in the workshop, typically about 20, and divide them into teams, half being the buyers and the other half the sellers. All of the buyers, and all of the sellers, receive identical sets of facts about themselves and the other side. They read them, meet one-on-one to negotiate, and, when they're finished, share the financial results of the negotiation with the group.

We then debrief both sides, in the process going over their goals for the negotiation, the CNAs for both sides, a power and Agreement Zone analysis, and their Wish Lists and subsequent trades. We then look at two aspects of each team's results: (1) the size of the pie, or the amount of value being divided, and (2) who claimed what percentage of that value. When we do, we usually find that in some pairs the buyer opened/anchored first, and in some the seller did. We also find that some of the opening offers were focused only on the price of the product or service for sale, while others took into account multiple trading variables, such as price, volume, length of contract, service, and so on. What's most important, though, is that we found, more often than not, that the teams that opened on just price and product were actually dividing a significantly smaller amount of money than those that anchored on numerous trades. Sometimes, in fact, those who opened the negotiation on a variety of items were actually creating and dividing as much as 50 percent more money than those who didn't.

When we subsequently analyze who got how much of a larger pie, we invariably find that it depends not only on how many items are included in the opening offers but on where those offers anchor the negotiation. In those instances in which either side anchored on one item and close to its own CNA, not only was the pie smaller than it could have been but the team also got less of the pie than those on the other side. When, instead, one side anchored closer to the other side's CNA, that side got more of the pie, but the pie still wasn't as large as it could have been. On the other hand, in those instances in which either side anchored on multiple items but still close to its own CNA, that side enlarged the pie but still got less of it. Finally, in those cases in which either side anchored on multiple items and close to the other side's CNA, not only was the pie larger but that side also got a bigger share of it. Thus, both what they anchored on and where they anchored affected the subsequent negotiation. This does not, however, just happen in our workshops. It happens in real life as well.

Here's another example of how anchoring can influence a negotiation. A few years ago, Margaret Neale, a professor at Stanford University and coauthor with Max Bazerman of *Negotiating Rationally* (Free Press, 1992), decided to test how the listing price of a house affected Realtors' estimations of its value. Selecting a house in Phoenix, Arizona, she first had it appraised to arrive at a listing price, then asked four groups of real estate brokers to evaluate the house. Each broker received a packet containing all the information brokers usually have to make such evaluations, including data on the house itself, the price of similar houses in the area, price per square foot, and so on and so on. There were, however, two differences in the packets the brokers received. In two of the groups' packets the listing price and the price per square foot were lower than the original appraisal, and in the other two groups' packets they were higher.

All the Realtors conducted walk-throughs of the house, did their calculations, and then presented the results. Although they all claimed, both before and after their presentations, that the listing price had little or no impact on their calculations, Professor Neale found, when the evaluations were presented, a direct correlation between the listing price and the Realtors' evaluations. The more money the Realtors thought the owner wanted for the house, the higher they assessed its worth. The point here is that anchoring—in this case on a price—can affect someone's thinking about the value of what's being negotiated and, accordingly, the subsequent negotiation.

Setting an Appropriate Anchor

For all of these reasons, it's extremely important for you to anchor the negotiation to your mutual advantage. During the validation meeting you should accordingly be looking for ways to provide anchors in two areas: (1) in trades that include items beyond just price and (2) in CNAs that include elements other than price. You can do this by asking carefully worded questions based on your estimations that enable you to shift and broaden the discussion beyond price alone.

If, for example, you think your customer is focused primarily on price, you might say something like: "I understand that price, warranties, service, and length of contract are important to you. How would you rank them most to least important?" By doing so, you can subtly set the tone for multiple trading items. Similarly, in regard to CNA, you might say to the customer: "In addition to a good price, how important is it to you that suppliers have the capacity to service you globally?" Assuming that you have a better global solution than your competitor (the customer's CNA), by raising this question you can find out how the customer feels and begin to subtly hint at the gap between what you and your competitor have to offer.

In our business, for example, many customers like to simply solicit a request for a proposal for negotiation training and ask us for our "price per person." In an effort to broaden the discussion beyond price, in our validation meetings we ask the client such anchoring questions as these:

- "How important is it to you to have custom case studies written specifically for your business?"
- "In addition to negotiation skills training, do you also want a negotiation 'strategy' or guidelines written at the corporate level that include individual negotiation parameters?"
- "Do you want individual coaching by our consultants to be available after the course is completed?"
- "Would you like to have your managers trained as in-house coaches for your salespeople?"
- "Would you like us to provide return on investment (ROI) information for the people who go through the course?"
- "Would you like to have a database that manages implementation of this negotiation initiative?"

Every one of these questions is directly related to items we want to include in a final deal—our Wish List. They are also all related to aspects of our value proposition that are typically not offered by our competition and therefore probably not included in the client's CNA Estimation. So by asking these questions, we can not only broaden the discussion beyond the zero-sum, single, price-per-head issue but also change the customer's CNA Estimation to the point where our offer is seen as radically different from our competitor's. In the process we also collect great data from our clients on how much they value each of these services, which provides us with information on potential trades. We also, of course, ask questions related to other elements of the deal, including length of contract, number of workshops, pricing, and so on.

But asking questions like these doesn't only enable you to start anchoring the negotiation. Based on your customer's responses, it also enables you to determine any untrue or inappropriate anchors, figure out where they are, and use that information to prepare your offers and prepare yourself for face-to-face trading in the final step of the process. Let's say, for example, that you're in a validation meeting with a buyer who tells you that his number one priority is a short-term, low purchase price. However, you've already met with the CFO, who told you that she's more concerned about the long-term, total cost of ownership. In that case, you know that either the buyer is bluffing or he's not aware of the larger and more strategic initiatives at the firm and is, accordingly, using an inappropriate and strategically useless anchor.

But the inappropriate anchor can be on your side as well. Let's say that you want to use a 50 percent gross margin as an anchor. Your cost is $25,000, so you try to sell your solution to a customer for $50,000. The only problem is that the client can build his own or buy the same solution from one of your competitor's for $35,000. In that case, your anchor is meaningless, unless you get lucky with an uneducated buyer. But even if you do, eventually they'll figure it out, and it will greatly damage your relationship.

• • • • •

Now, before I go on to discuss the operational aspects of the validation meeting itself, you should think about the live negotiation that you've been focusing on throughout the book and try to determine if you and your customer have already become anchored in a way that might be either a hindrance or a help in this negotiation. Again, remember that anchors can exist in a wide variety of areas, including price, contract clauses, product-service mix, and the like. Remember, too, that your industry may be anchored in some way. For example, it might be standard practice in your business for sellers to give away a variety of customer services, so it would be a good idea to note any such anchors below so that you'll be able to keep them in mind when you conduct your validation meeting:

1. _____
2. _____
3. _____
4. _____

THE VALIDATION MEETING

There are essentially five elements that you need to take into account when planning and conducting a validation meeting. These include:

1. Setting up meetings
2. Asking questions and listening
3. Sharing/Trading data and answering questions from the other side
4. Avoiding things you shouldn't do
5. Evaluating the success of a validation meeting

Setting Up Meetings

When you're in the negotiation phase of a sale and ask to meet with a customer, the customer typically thinks you're coming in to "sell" them or to start price negotiations. There is, of course, a good reason for them to think that—it's what usually happens. So given that history, it's extremely important in setting up a validation meeting to establish a clear objective and make sure your customer understands what that objective is.

Before you do that, though, determine exactly with whom you want to meet. If, in your sales process, you called on multiple influential buyers in the customer's organization, you absolutely need to call on those same individuals—not only buyers but influential managers as well—during the negotiation process. Because a number of individuals may be involved in the process as a result, you may end up with several small meetings rather than one large group meeting. You may also, at this point, encounter resistance from some of those individuals concerning the time required to attend a meeting. I have found, though, that if a customer won't agree to a face-to-face meeting, more often than not they will agree to a telephone call, particularly if you promise to keep it to no more than 15 minutes and to send the questions in advance.

The advantage of negotiating at multiple levels within the customer's organization is that the more influential buyers and managers you speak with, the more customer needs you can learn about and address. If, for example, you only interview a buyer, all you may hear is "I want the lowest price." At the same time, if you interview a senior vice president, you may learn that the customer is also interested in your bringing your solution to both their domestic and their international operations. The more you know about what the customer really needs, the easier it will be to create trades and, ultimately, more value.

The way I usually handle this is to send the client an e-mail asking for an appointment and providing the following information:

- The purpose of the meeting is to find out the client's needs as they relate to the upcoming negotiation.
- I will primarily be asking questions that allow me to formulate an offer, one that speaks to the client's needs, sometime after the meeting.
- I will *not* be presenting price or product at the meeting.
- Some of the questions I'll ask include these:
  - What specific items should we focus on in the negotiation?
  - How important is each of these items?
  - What are some target metrics for each of these items?
  - How do you view the supplier landscape in our marketplace?
  - What are the strengths and weaknesses of those suppliers?
  - What would you like suppliers to do that they don't?

By providing this kind of information to your customers before the meeting, it makes it clear to them that you're not going to be making a sales pitch or getting started in what is traditionally thought of as negotiations. Perhaps even more important, it makes it clear that you are genuinely interested in understanding their needs, even though in fact these meetings provide you with an enormous tactical benefit. It can also help you avoid situations—which we've occasionally run into ourselves—in which validation meetings backfire because management-level customers come to meetings expecting to learn more about our services, find us asking a lot of questions, and go away frustrated.

Asking Questions and Listening

I imagine you've heard the old 80/20 rule to guide your listening and speaking, respectively. This couldn't be more important in a validation meeting. Virtually the only time you should speak is either to ask a question, to follow up on a question, or to trade specific data from your side. Remember that the primary purpose of this meeting is to gain information, so the less you talk and the more you listen, the more you will accomplish.

The questions you ask, of course, are the CNA-related and Wish List–related questions you prepared earlier in the validation step of the process. I've found that it's advantageous to ask the questions as systematically as possible—to stick to your plan but not be so rigid that you can't explore unexpected opportunities. In terms of what questions to ask first, I suggest that you open the meeting by revisiting the purpose of the meeting as outlined in your invitation, then ask Wish List–related questions, and only then CNA-related questions

Although, as you'll recall, you prepared the CNA questions before the Wish List ones, I've found that most people are much more willing to share what they want (their Wish List) than what happens if they don't reach agreement with you (their CNA). Asking Wish List questions first, then, gets everybody loosened up and talking. In fact, if you look back at the sample questions I suggested you include in the e-mail to your customer, you'll see that they're divided into two groups, the first having to do with Wish List items and the second with CNA. Of course, when you get to the meeting, your questions will be much more targeted and will have your initial estimations embedded in them.

For example, rather than simply asking the generic Wish List question "What specific items should we focus on in the negotiation?" you would say, "It's my understanding you want to focus on price, volume, length of contract, and service agreements in the upcoming negotiation. Is that right? Is there anything missing? Is there anything that should be deleted?" Similarly, instead of asking the generic CNA question "How do you view the supplier landscape in our marketplace?" you might say, "I understand that if you don't choose us for your partner on this initiative, you'll choose ABC Corporation. Is that right?" Again, by asking the questions in this way, you show the customer that you've done your homework, and you're likely to get answers that are of more value in developing trades.

Regardless of how you phrase your questions, however, it's important to try to keep your tone as conversational as possible. Even though your questions have actually been very well thought out and designed to both solicit and share information, people get nervous if they feel you're "filling out a form" and can become self-conscious about what they say. Keeping the conversation as casual as possible helps to ensure a freer flow of information in both directions.

Finally, I suggest that you write down what the customer tells you. There are actually two schools of thought on this. The first claims that people are likely to be more guarded if you write down what they say. The other school argues that your taking notes makes the speaker feel that you value what he or she is saying and consider it important. My experience suggests that the latter is almost invariably true; recording what customers say doesn't seem to inhibit them at all. Moreover, if there's more than one person on your side in the meeting, having written notes makes it easier to compare what you heard when you begin the next step in the process.

Sharing/Trading Data and Answering Questions from the Other Side

If you're going to ask customers to provide information during a validation meeting about what they want, it's only natural for them to expect you to reciprocate. In other words, you have to give something to get something. Of course, the idea of sharing information is often counterintuitive for both sides, as many of us have been taught to "keep your cards close to your chest" in a negotiation. Needless to say, it's going to be very difficult to trade data if either you or your client take that approach. In fact, the only way that both of you can get a deal better than your CNA and realize as many of your Wish List items as possible is by sharing that information with each other. In fact, the most value-creating agreements we've seen are those in which both sides openly share data on their Wish Lists.

Although the likelihood of that happening in your first validation meeting is slim, the more meetings you have with a customer in which you demonstrate your desire to create joint value, the more the customer will trust you and consequently be willing to share data. The results of a recent study by the consulting firm A.T. Kearney bear this out. After analyzing trust in high-level business alliances and the effect it had on relationships and profits for both parties, the firm reported two findings, among others, that are of particular significance here. The first was that trust is built between parties based on their actions over time. The second was that a direct correlation exists between trust and profit. What that means in terms of validation meetings is that if you consistently share data with customers, not only will trust go up but so too will the quality of your agreements and your profits. Again, it may take several negotiations to develop this trust, but it pays off.

But sharing information doesn't only help build trust in a general sense. It can also help you get your customer to share information during the meeting itself. Look at it this way. If I come up and yell at you, there's a good chance that you'll yell back. But if I'm nice and polite to you, there's a good chance you'll be equally nice and polite to me. It's the same with trading data. Let's say, for example, that you say to a customer "I understand price, volume, and length of contract are the key items you're interested in negotiating," and the customer stonewalls you. If you share the same list for your side, and can show the customer that you're willing to trust them, so you're much more likely to get a meaningful response when you go back later and ask the same question again.

The next question, then, is what should and shouldn't be shared in a validation meeting. Here are some guidelines, going from the safest to the riskiest:

- Share the Wish List items you would like to negotiate.
- Share your ranking of those items.
- Share your weighting of those items.
- Share the high end of your range for those items.
- Share aspects of your CNA.

You obviously must be willing to share the items on your Wish List with your customer because if you don't you'll have nothing with which to trade. But you should give out information about rank, weight, and ranges a little bit at a time, in that order, and in exchange for information from the other side. CNA information should be shared sparingly, because it's from CNA data that the low end of your Agreement Zone can be diagnosed and the power analysis completed, both of which would provide your customer with an advantage over you.

There are, however, instances in which sharing your CNA information can be beneficial. Let's say, for example, that you're in a validation meeting and your customer is telling you that they're looking for your solution at a price that's 50 percent lower than your average market yield. At the moment, though, the demand for your services is high. In that kind of situation it may be in your best interest to share those data with them. In addition, "leaking" this kind of information can serve to alert the customer to what to expect in the final proposal and subsequent negotiation.

Avoiding Things You Shouldn't Do

In addition to those things you should do in a validation meeting, there are, of course, things you shouldn't do. Principal among these are those things you promised your customer you wouldn't do when you asked for the meeting—start "negotiating" (i.e., discussing terms) or "selling." Sometimes it's hard to not do these things. When, for example, you hear something crazy from the other side in regard to a particular item you've asked about, it's difficult to not start trading over that item or trying to correct an incorrect anchor. But emotional or tactical reactions like those serve only to stop the flow of information from them to you. And that's the last thing you want to do at this point. Moreover, although ultimately you *will* be haggling over terms, this is not the time to do it, if for no other reason than that you don't have enough information yet. The only exception to this might be when you are using the process to blueprint a negotiation in real time, that is, you're involved in a nonstrategic negotiation or one in which there's not very much money involved and you're going to go through the whole process in one sitting. But even in that kind of situation you should hold off beginning to prepare and present your offer until you feel you've learned enough to do so.

"Selling" during a validation meeting is equally counterproductive. Even if the customer seems to want you to sell him or her—and sometimes they do—you prepared for and promised something else, so you should stick to your promise. As with "negotiating," if, having said you want to listen, you proceed to just talk, all you'll accomplish is to keep the other side from providing you with the information you supposedly came for. Perhaps even more important, when you tell a customer that you're there to understand their needs and you start selling, you can do serious damage to your credibility as well as to any hope of building trust between you. And without that trust, there is no hope of getting the customer to share the information you need to develop value-creating offers.

Evaluating the Success of a Validation Meeting

Conducting a validation meeting is essentially the same as doing market research. When you do that kind of research, you always start with an end in mind—the kind of information you're hoping to gather. So, as with any market research effort, you measure the success of a validation meeting by the extent to which you've learned what you set out to learn. Of course, in this case what you're hoping to learn is more about the customer's CNA, the positive and negative effects of that CNA, and the customer's Wish List of items.

Remember that the main purpose of blueprinting a negotiation is simply to answer two questions: What are the consequences if we do not reach agreement? and What items are likely to be included if we do reach agreement? Your estimations, the internal and external validations, and the questions you prepared for this meeting were all designed to give you and the customer a clearer picture of the blueprint. So the more capable you've become of answering those two questions, the more you've been able to blueprint the negotiation, the more successful you've been, and the more successful you'll be in the remaining steps of the negotiation.

But there's another means of gauging success in a validation meeting, one that's a bit more difficult to measure but also extremely important. Aside from enabling you to gather data about the other side, the validation meeting provides you with an opportunity to help your customers become more rational about their own CNA and organize their desired trades. So even if a customer doesn't answer your questions, the fact that you asked the questions—particularly when you've embedded your estimations into them—can start them thinking about their CNA as well as about items other than just price. This is essentially a proactive anchoring approach that's beneficial to both sides.

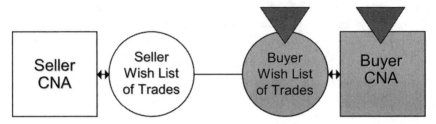

As I've mentioned, most people still think of the face-to-face presentation of offers as the most important tactical aspect of "negotiating." But whether the validation meeting is a 15-minute phone call with one buyer or several meetings with several buyers at multiple management levels, it is vastly more important than that final discussion. That's why preparing good estimations, embedding those estimations into thoughtful questions, posing those questions in a logical sequence, and listening to and recording the answers can make a difference not only between impasse and agreement but, even more important, between "win-win" and value-creating negotiations.

B *est* P *ractices* R *eview*

- Invite multiple levels of buyers.
- Make the meeting objective clear.
- Don't get defensive; collect more information.
- Learn about the other side's view of their CNA and Wish List.
- Anchor through asking questions and sharing data on your CNA and Wish List.

Common Mistakes to Avoid

- Asking unnecessary questions that inflame or irrelevant questions that don't provide CNA or Wish List data.
- Getting defensive in reaction to a tactic from the other side rather than seeking to understand it.
- Trying to make trades or sell during the validation meeting.

• • • • •

Now, having validated your estimations in a meeting with your customer, you will probably be happy, if perhaps surprised, to learn that the bulk of the hard work involved in blueprinting a negotiation is done. Of course, many people think of the steps you've just completed as planning and the next steps as tactics, or what's traditionally considered "negotiating." But, again, as far as I'm concerned, it's *all* negotiating. In fact, developing the Consequences of No Agreement and Wish List Estimations, and validating those estimations by doing internal and public data searches, and meeting with your customer, are not only part of negotiation but are perhaps the most important part. That's not to say, however, that even though the next two steps require less effort that they're not important. Without them you can't conclude the kind of value-generating deal that you want for both sides. In fact, creating value is exactly what the next step is about.

STEP THREE
USING THE BLUEPRINT
TO CREATE VALUE

Now that you've completed the first two steps of our Strategic Negotiation Process—Estimating the Blueprint and Validating the Estimation—it's time to go on to Step Three: Using the Blueprint to Create Value.

Estimate	Validate	Create Value	Divide Value
⊕ CNA ⊕ Wish List of Trades	⊕ In-House/Public Sources ⊕ Meeting Preparation ⊕ Validation Meeting	⊕ **Exceed CNAs** ⊕ **Look for Trades**	⊕ Anchor on MEO ⊕ Trading ⊕ Claim Value

You began this process by establishing a negotiation goal to "create joint value and divide it given concerns for fairness in the ongoing relationship." And, as you've seen, numerous small steps are involved in attaining that goal. But all the work you've done so far has been engineered to bring you to this point—the point at which you can actually begin to create value, which you do in two ways.

First, you do it by putting a deal on the table that, if agreed to, leaves both you and your customer better off than your alternatives to agreeing—your CNAs. This can be difficult because many times you find yourself across the table from a buyer who either hasn't truly diagnosed their CNA or, worse yet, has misdiagnosed it and believes that it's better, faster, or cheaper than it really is.

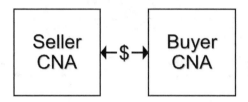

Second, you create value by trading as many prioritized Wish List items as possible so you can "expand the pie" that's being negotiated and therefore create more value for both sides to divide. This is also difficult to accomplish because, more often than not, either one or both sides hasn't even taken the time to think through all the items up for negotiation, much less rank which are most to least important. In addition, even those customers who have thought through what they want are more than likely to keep that information close to the chest.

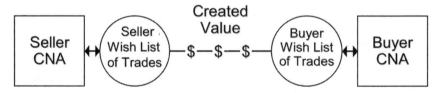

Nonetheless, having estimated and validated your own and your customer's most likely CNA and Wish Lists, you already have a great deal of information about your customer, very possibly even more than they do. Moreover, you're now much closer to answering the two questions that need to be answered if you want to create and divide value between you and your customer: What are the consequences if we do not reach agreement? and What items are likely to be included if we do reach agreement? And, most important, having gathered that information, you've shifted the balance in your favor and are now in a position to make use of that information to begin preparing the kind of offers that will enable you to attain your goal.

DEVELOPING MULTIPLE EQUAL OFFERS

Note that I've used the word *offers* because, in fact, the end result of this step will be not one offer that you can make to your customer but rather two to four of what we call Multiple Equal Offers (MEOs). These are essentially offers that are of approximately equal value to you but should be of varying value to those on the other side. These offers are also custom made because they're based on the CNA and Wish Lists you've estimated and validated for both sides in each deal. And they are all designed to provide each side with something better than its Consequences of No Agreement, and to include as many trades as possible, so as to increase the value to both sides.

Although Multiple Equal Offers may sound somewhat like "bundles," they're actually different for several reasons. Bundles are typically offered "off the shelf" rather than customized for a particular deal. They are also typically not packaged to benefit both sides but rather to benefit the seller by loading in high-margin or slow-moving items or services. And, finally, when a bundle is offered, there's usually only one rather than two to four, as is the case with MEOs.

But exactly how do you develop these offers? You do it by using the data you've gathered in the two previous steps on your own and your customer's Wish List and Consequences of No Agreement.

Using the Wish List Estimation

By now you will have gathered a great deal of information about both the items on your Wish List and the items on your customer's Wish List and the relative importance of those items to each of you. At this point, in order to use that information to create joint value, you have to look closely at those items and determine two things. The first is which items are on your list but not on your customer's, and vice versa. The second is the relative importance to you and to your customer of the items that are on your lists. It is these differences that make it possible for you to trade and, in the process, create value. For example, your customer may want you to warehouse their purchase, something which may be of little importance to you. When you develop your offers, then, you can include that item in one of them. But because this is about trading, if you offer warehousing to your customer, you will also include something in the offer that's important to you, such as a longer contract.

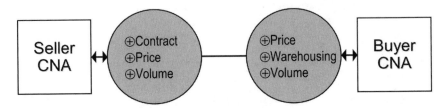

Trading is not, however, only about *adding* items. In the course of gathering information you may, for example, learn that your customer doesn't want a certain clause in the agreement, such as a raw materials clause, which makes them responsible for increased raw materials costs. In that situation, it would be taking something out of one of the MEOs that acts as a trade. Again, though, if you take that clause out, you will add something of greater value to you, such as increased volume or an introduction to a new division. The point here is that it's essential that you look closely at the items on your Wish List and your customer's, determine where the differences lie, and make use of those differences to build value by embedding trades into your Multiple Equal Offers.

You don't necessarily, however, have to restrict yourself to items on the lists. There may well be additional items that are not officially on the table but that you can introduce in order to create even more joint value. You'll recall the story I told earlier about the insurance company and the home improvement retailer who were negotiating the price-per-yard of replacement carpeting to be used by the insurance company's policyholders. The buyer and seller were negotiating hard over price and, despite having considered a large number of possible trades, had almost reached an impasse. By creatively brainstorming every conceivable trade, however, they eventually landed on "trading tapes" of their consumer databases and creating some joint marketing. This very creative trade not only saved both sides money by eliminating the necessity of purchasing additional databases, it also resulted in new revenue streams for both.

This example explains why I would encourage you to look for trades beyond what's on the table now. In exchange for something your customer considers important, you might, for example, ask for access to the customer's business in countries where you don't now have access or ask for the opportunity to sell a product or service that the customer isn't currently buying from you. Suggesting such items can be particularly helpful when you learn from your validation that the customer is looking for something very aggressive from you, such as free service calls or deeply discounted pricing. In fact, it's often this kind of creative offer that can make the difference between impasse and agreement.

Using the CNA Estimation

In the same way that you embed information from your Wish List Estimations into your MEOs, you should embed information from your CNA Estimations. Doing so, at least for your own side, isn't particularly difficult. Because your most likely CNA is to lose the business, the effects of the CNA are that you will either have to replace this business with a new customer or get more business from an existing customer. Your CNA will accordingly look better or worse depending on the market demand for your product or service and the average market price for what you sell. For that reason, you should make sure when you develop your MEOs that they provide you with something that's greater than your CNA. In fact, the only time you should go below the current market yield for your product or service is when there is what one of our consultants calls "a compelling trade," that is, a trade that has value in excess of what you're giving up. As I mentioned earlier, we have on occasion traded heavily for nontraditional items, such as experience in a new market, when doing so provided us with something that was of greater value to us, such as, in this case, creating a new revenue stream.

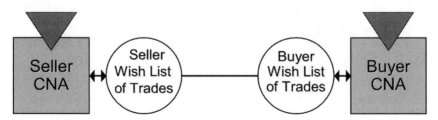

Making use of the other side's CNA Estimation is, however, somewhat more difficult. But it can be done, and you do it by looking at what we refer to as the Gap. The Gap, which you typically find after completing the CNA estimation and validation for a customer, is the difference between your understanding of what the customer needs and wants and what the customer can get by going to one of your competitors, doing it themselves, or doing nothing at all—that is, their CNA. If there is no Gap, the negotiation is going to be difficult for one very good reason—if you can't tell the customer why your offer is better than their CNA, how can you expect them to choose you? In fact, if you find yourself in that kind of position, you've either not done a very good job of analyzing the situation or you have a value proposition problem. Fortunately, assuming it's not a value proposition problem, the analysis can be done again. But it is, in any case, your responsibility to find that Gap. In fact, the Gap is the Holy Grail of CNA analysis! It's the entire reason you take the time to do this work and probably the most important aspect of any negotiation.

In every successful negotiation we've ever been part of, we have found and—even more important—exploited a CNA Gap. For example, earlier I told you about one of our clients that specialized in data management services. They found themselves in a situation in which one of their customers believed that its CNA—building its own database—would be better, faster, and cheaper than buying what it said were the outrageously expensive services of our client. When we did the CNA analysis, however, we found huge gaps between what the customer needed and wanted and the customer's CNA.

For one, although the customer believed that building their own database would be better because they'd be able to customize it, we realized that, by doing so, they wouldn't be able to integrate their new database into the old one. We also realized that even though they thought they could do it faster themselves, it would actually take twice as long as they anticipated because they hadn't considered many of the steps that had to be taken. Nor would it be cheaper, even though they thought it would, because they had neglected to take into account the cost of the ongoing maintenance of the database. In addition, building their own database would expose them to enormous risks. If it took longer, was more expensive, and/or didn't provide the high-quality reports they needed, they couldn't blame it on a supplier and would therefore have to take the heat themselves. Needless to say, when our client presented its customer with its offers, they made sure that the client understood how its offers were better than the customer's CNA. Of course, you may not always find the kind of huge Gap we did here, but there has to be at least one or the negotiation will stall.

One place where you might be able to exploit a Gap is in the area of *incumbency,* a huge issue in CNA analysis, as noted earlier. Although I hesitate to state the obvious here, if you're a successful incumbent and the customer will have to remove you from their organization if they choose someone else—a cost associated with their CNA—you already have a huge power advantage. But the reverse is also true. If you're negotiating against a successful incumbent, one benefit of the client's CNA—staying with the incumbent—is their ability to avoid the hassle associated with switching suppliers. On the other hand, if the incumbent has not been servicing the customer well and you can offer better service, you can exploit that Gap and help both the customer and yourself. Remember, if you can't clearly show the customer how your offer is better than their CNA, closing will be difficult, if not impossible.

Let me give you an example of what I'm talking about. One of our consultants, Steve Thompson, is a former naval officer who lived in Chicago when he was single and enjoyed sailing his 30-foot boat on Lake Michigan. But when Steve and his girlfriend, Jan, decided to get married and move to Atlanta, he realized that he had to sell his sailboat to make a down payment on a new house. So he listed the sailboat in the papers and at the local sailing clubs in Chicago with an asking price of $32,000. The price included an extra, beautiful teal blue sail as well as a hand-crafted stainless steel storage rack for an inflatable safety boat (also included), which Steve had designed and built himself.

Several buyers came and went until, finally, two couples—two brothers and their wives—came to see the boat and were serious about buying it. They particularly loved the look of the extra colorful sail because it made the boat stand out. There was, however, a problem: the absolute maximum they could pay for the boat was $25,000. Having already blueprinted the negotiation, Steve was prepared to come down to $27,000 if he could keep the extra sail and safety boat and rack. He knew that he would get another boat once he got settled in his new life and he'd be able to use them.

So during a meeting on the boat with the two couples, Steve suggested the lower price. Unfortunately, even though the couples agreed that it was fair, they had two problems with it. First, it was still $2,000 higher than their budget and, second, although they didn't care about the safety boat and storage rack, they loved the colorful sail. Steve, in turn, offered to sell them the boat and the sail for $28,000, but, much as they were clearly tempted, it was still over their budget. Reluctantly, both sides agreed to accept their CNAs—Steve to find another buyer and the couples to find another boat.

But it was a beautiful Sunday afternoon and because they were all on the boat anyway, Steve invited them for a sail. While sailing, Steve realized that none of these people had sailing experience. In fact, they told him, the reason they only had $25,000 for the boat was that they had saved $30,000, but $5,000 of that was budgeted for sailing lessons! Obviously, a boat's not much good if no one knows how to sail it. But that was the piece of information Steve needed. Not only is he a former naval officer, but he's also a licensed sailing instructor. So he offered to sell them the boat with the colorful sail and four sailing certifications for $29,000, and they immediately accepted. In the meantime, Steve got to keep the safety boat, which, while not important to the couples, was important to him.

What Steve did, then, was to give the buyers several choices:

* The sailboat with no extra sail and no safety boat ($27,000)
* The sailboat with the extra sail but without the safety boat ($28,000)
* The sailboat with the extra sail and four certifications but without the safety boat ($29,000)
* The sailboat with the extra sail and the safety boat ($30,000)

All of these deals were acceptable to Steve because they were all equal to him in terms of his return. But the third deal was the best for both sides. Steve got to keep the safety boat and storage rack as well as making $1,000 more than he had anticipated. The couples got the boat, the extra sail, and the certifications they needed for $1,000 less than they'd anticipated. In other words, all the parties, by trading, were able to increase the value of the deal and then divide it between them. (In fact, Steve got an added benefit. He was selling the boat at the start of the season because prices and demand would drop had he waited until the fall. But that meant that he'd have to spend his last summer in Chicago without a sailboat. Now, giving the couples lessons, he would be out sailing almost all summer on a boat someone else had to maintain!)

Structuring the Deal

But exactly how do you structure Multiple Equal Offers? Here's an example of how we do it in our own business. When we're trying to sell our negotiation solution to a prospective customer, we often hear from buyers that what they're most interested in is the lowest price per head. At the same time, when we talk to higher-level executives in the buyer's company, they often say what they want is a negotiation process that's customized and truly integrated into their organization. In order to accommodate both parties, what we usually do is provide three Multiple Equal Offers:

1. A high-priced, high-value custom solution
2. A very low-priced, off-the-shelf package
3. Something in between

Of course, if a customer says they only have $50,000 to spend, we always offer them a $50,000 solution. But it's typically the lowest priced off-the-shelf solution we offer. At the same time, we offer a fully customized solution with all the bells and whistles. Perhaps not surprisingly, when we present these different options to the buyer and someone at the executive level, more often than not the executive quickly discounts the low-priced, stripped-down version as something that won't work for their organization and takes it off the list for us. In fact, we usually end up throwing out both the highest-priced and the lowest-priced solution and settling on the middle deal, which is typically the best for both of us.

Typical MEOs would look something like this:

	Sample Multiple Equal Offers		
Item	**Option 1: Long-Term Strategic Alliance**	**Option 2: Long-Term Strategic Relationship**	**Option 3: Short-Term Flexible Relationship**
Price	$14/unit	$12/unit	$10/unit
Length	3 years	1 year	Quarterly commitments
Volume	4,000 units	2,000 units	1,000 units
Support	7 days/week in person	5 days/week in person	5 days/week by phone
Payment Terms	45 days	30 days	Upon receipt

You'll note that as the unit price, length of contract, and number of units go down from the first to the third option, so too do the value-added services and support we provide. Looking at it from the opposite side, you'll see that as unit price, length of contract, and units go up, so does our commitment to more service. In addition, as potential revenues increase from the third to the first option, we are also willing to take on more risk in payment terms.

You should also note that I've labeled each of these offers in terms of different *relationships.* In today's business environment, it's much more likely that you're selling business relationships than price and product. By presenting these offers in terms of relationships, then, you've shifted your negotiations to bring them into line with your sales process. In other words, you're selling *and* negotiating your value proposition in the form of different business relationships. You'll also note that it's usually best, as we do, to offer three different relationships. Except in very simple deals, two relationships don't really provide enough flexibility, and four can get too confusing. Three seems to be the optimal number.

Finally, just as it's important to consult with others in your organization during the estimation and validation steps of blueprinting a negotiation, it's also important to consult with them during this step of the process. If you work in a company in which you have to interact with lawyers concerning legal terms, finance people concerning payment terms, product managers concerning product pricing, and/or service managers concerning service pricing, all of them should be included in the construction of these MEOs. Let's say, for example, that your lawyers want to shift all the legal risk to the other side—which is, of course, what lawyers are paid to do—but you know that your customer is extremely risk averse. In that case, you can work with the lawyers to develop two or three different offers in which you can decrease your customer's risk while increasing your return. Working with all the stakeholders in your organization provides you with two very important benefits. First, it gives you the option of trading and creating value internally. And, second, it enables you to gain the trust and respect of internal stakeholders, which can be important in advancing your career.

Structuring Your Own Multiple Equal Offers (MEOs)

Now that you understand how MEOs are structured, it's time for you to develop drafts for three Multiple Equal Offers for your own negotiation. At this point you may not have yet had the opportunity to validate your CNA and Wish List Estimations, so if that's the case this will be a practice run. You can start practicing by going back to the Wish List Estimations you developed for both yourself and your customer in Chapter 5 and looking again at, first, which items are on your list and your customer's, second, the relative importance to you and your customer of those items, and, third, the desired ranges for each potential trade.

The Wish List item that is most important to each side should give you a sense of the two "outer" offers, one in which you get your lead item and the other in which your customer gets theirs. You can then develop a third option that's somewhere between the two. You should also look at the differences in the high and low ranges for possible trades. If, for example, there's an item on which you and your customer are far apart, you can build one offer that provides your customer with what they want and compensates you, and another offer in which you get what you want and compensates your customer.

Once you've finished your analysis of the Wish List Estimations, you have to go back to the CNA Estimations you developed for yourself and your customer in Chapter 4. Look at them closely to see if you can find the Gap between what you can provide your customer and what they can get from going to one of your competitors, doing it themselves, or doing nothing. If, for example, you know that your ability to customize your solution makes what you have to offer better than the customer's alternative to reaching agreement with you (their CNA), you can build one offer that's called "Highly-Customized Relationship," and build that customization into the trades. You should pay attention, too, to your own alternatives, particularly things like market demand, pricing, and profitability. By doing so you'll be able to develop offers that close the Gap for the customer and, at the same time, provide you with more than you can get elsewhere. Finally, once you've analyzed both the Wish List and CNA Estimations, you should complete the development of your MEOs in the space on page 140.

Rehearsing Your Presentation

Now that you've developed your MEOs, before you go on to present them to your customer, it's important for you to rehearse your presen-

---

YOUR MULTIPLE EQUAL OFFERS

Item	Option 1: _____	Option 2: _____	Option 3: _____
	_____	_____	_____
	_____	_____	_____
1. _____	_____	_____	_____
2. _____	_____	_____	_____
3. _____	_____	_____	_____
4. _____	_____	_____	_____
5. _____	_____	_____	_____
6. _____	_____	_____	_____
7. _____	_____	_____	_____

---

tation with all the people on your side who will be attending the meeting with the customer. There are essentially three things to focus on when rehearsing:

1. *Providing an overview of the MEOs.* This means naming each of the offers in terms of different relationships and briefly explaining what each includes before going into details. This presentation provides your customer with a good general idea of the alternatives and the differences among them. Setting up the three MEOs is probably even more important than the details of each.

2. *Making certain that you're clear on the CNA Gap.* This means having no question in your mind about why what you have to offer is better than your customer's CNA, as well as your own. If you're unsure about this in any way, you might not be able to make the kind of forceful argument you may need to make in order to close the deal. Keep in mind that a customer will take your offer so long as it's at least marginally better than the alternative, so the first thing you have to do is diplomatically educate the customer on exactly how it is better.

3. *Making sure your customer can see that you've used the information you gathered in the validation meeting to build joint value.* Making it clear that you've done all you could to ensure that you will both get a deal that's better than your CNA and one that includes as many

important trades as possible will go a long way toward making your customer receptive to your offers.

B est P r a c t i c e s R e v i e w

- Build custom MEOs for every deal based on both sides' CNA and Wish Lists.
- Exploit the Gap between your customer's needs and their alternative by addressing it effectively in your MEOs.
- Title each offer in terms of relationship or value, not price.

C o m m o n M i s t a k e s t o A v o i d

- Building in nonmeasurable trades, such as "relationship."
- Developing too many MEOs or including so much data that it gets confusing.
- Forgetting to focus on the needs of both sides in creating your MEOs.

· · · · ·

By this point you've moved very far along in blueprinting a negotiation by developing a goal to "create joint value and divide it given concerns for fairness in the ongoing relationship," conducting Consequences of No Agreement and Wish List Estimations for both sides in the negotiation, validating those estimations by using public sources, asking questions of colleagues and soliciting information from your customer, and using all the information you've gathered to prepare the offers you will make. The next and final step—Dividing Value—focuses on presenting the MEOs and handling the tactical aspects of trading, bluffing, impasse, and, ultimately, closing, all of which are covered in the next chapter.

10

STEP FOUR
USING THE BLUEPRINT
TO DIVIDE VALUE

Now, having estimated both your own and your customer's CNA and Wish Lists, validated your estimations, and created value by constructing Multiple Equal Offers for your customer, it's time to go on to the fourth and final step in the Strategic Negotiation Process: Using the Blueprint to Divide Value.

Estimate	Validate	Create Value	Divide Value
⊕ CNA	⊕ In-House/Public Sources	⊕ Exceed CNAs	⊕ **Anchor on MEO**
⊕ Wish List of Trades	⊕ Meeting Preparation	⊕ Look for Trades	⊕ **Trading**
	⊕ Validation Meeting		⊕ **Claim Value**

Actually, talking about this step in such terms isn't entirely accurate, even though that is ultimately what happens. This is the step that most people think of as "negotiating," but what it's really about is *trading*. As such, it's what all the work you've done up to this point is for. This is where it pays off. It's the same as if, instead of learning a new way to negotiate, you had learned to play an instrument, studied and rehearsed, auditioned for and won a chair in a symphony orchestra, and were now about to play for the first time. As in that kind of situation, you might feel a little nervous, but you'll soon find that you're prepared for anything your listener—or your customer—might throw at you.

You'll recall that in the chapter on setting up and running validation meetings I discussed opening offers and other anchors. I also mentioned how you can use your validation questions to begin some subtle anchoring on both multiple trading items and CNA analyses that include elements other than price. Now, having developed Multiple Equal Offers for your customer, you've built on that concept by anchoring on three different business relationships, each with multiple variables. And because you have, it's extremely unlikely that you will end up negotiating only price. What will probably happen when you sit down to present the MEOs to your customer is the customer will want to anchor on "price and product," while you will want to anchor on the "total value" of your business solution. And, in fact, all the work you've done up to this point has put you in a good position to do that.

I must point out, however, as I've said before, that there are no guarantees here. In the words of my partner, Max Bazerman, "There are no silver bullets for negotiation, but a good process shifts the odds in your favor." So I can't absolutely promise that using the Strategic Negotiation Process will enable you to conduct successful negotiations every time. What I can promise you is that doing so will greatly increase the odds of your being able to take a proactive role in managing the negotiation rather than a reactive and tactical one, and that, as a result, you will be surprised less often, you'll have more power, and most of the negotiations you're involved in will produce a high degree of joint value.

Now, before I begin to discuss the mechanics of the presentation of your MEOs, one important point needs to be made. We're often asked who should open first in a negotiation; there are two schools of thought. The first school contends that you should let the other side open first so they'll show their hand. The second says that you should open first so you can anchor the negotiation. But the right answer to the question: "It depends."

In a situation in which you're rolling out a brand-new service, you're not sure exactly how it will be valued, and you don't have good data on the other side's Wish List and CNA, it would probably be best to float the concept out there a little and let the market value it by opening first. Alternatively, you may have a product or service that's been available for some time with a well-established selling price, and have good data on the customer's Wish List, the costs and benefits associated with their CNA, and the resultant Gap. In that kind of situation, it would be appropriate for you to open so you can anchor first and marginally better than their CNA, and on as many trades as possible. Ultimately, doing so will allow you to claim most of the Agreement Zone.

THE MULTIPLE EQUAL OFFERS PRESENTATION

As with the validation meeting, the first thing you must do in regard to the MEO presentation is determine who should be there. In extending invitations, it's advantageous to include as many of those individuals with whom you've had validation meetings or phone conversations as possible. This is important because, even though lower-level buying influences are usually more concerned with price, those on the executive level tend to be more interested in a comprehensive package, which is, of course, what you really want to sell. So if you've successfully used your sales process to sell the total value of your solution and continued to do so through the negotiation process, it's likely that if those executives attend the meeting, the lowest-priced, low-value MEO will almost immediately be discarded. If you can't get executive-level buying influences to the presentation but have completed validation calls with them, it's important when you review the MEOs that you let the buyer know that the senior vice president—or whoever—was particularly interested in X, Y, and Z in an offer, and that you designed such-and-such an MEO with his or her needs in mind.

When you do begin your presentation, you should start with an overview of the three offers. Remember that it's important in the overview to include the title of each of the offers so your customer can immediately recognize the type of relationship between your companies that each offer represents. Once you've outlined all three, it's best to start with the lowest-priced option, review the details, go on to the highest-priced option, and then finish with the one in the middle. This option is typically the best for both sides, and you should make that clear to your customer by showing them how it includes as many of their Wish List items as possible—citing what they told you during the validation step—as well as how it meets your own needs. Doing this benefits both of you in two ways. First, it shows the customer that this is the best option based entirely on facts, not emotions. And, second, by explaining how it meets your needs as well, it shows them that you're being honest, which helps foster trust between you.

Once you've made the presentation of the three MEOs, the next step is to launch your attack—in a diplomatic way—on their Consequences of No Agreement in order to exploit the Gap you identified during your analysis. Like me, you may have been taught that you should always upsell your own solution and not speak ill of competitors. Let's get this straight, though. This is business, the best wins, and this is exactly the right time to attack their CNA—whether it's your competition, doing it themselves, or doing nothing. This is what closing is all about. Of course, no one likes to be "closed." But businesspeople do want to make the best decision to meet their needs. And it's your job as a consultative salesperson to helpfully let your customer know why your middle Multiple Equal Offer is much better than their alternative (their CNA) and that it trades on many items that they ranked as important. Here's an example of the kind of thing we say when we want to do that with one of our own customers:

> When I came to see you a few days ago to learn about what you wanted, I got a lot of very valuable information, and I've embedded that information into my second offer. For example, you mentioned that customization and the ability to implement an organizationwide process are important to you. Now, one of the other things I learned at our meeting is that you're considering two of our competitors, ACME Negotiating and Professor So-and-So from the University of Wherever. If you don't choose us, I'd suggest you choose ACME, as they're the best of our competitors. Professor So-and-So's primary function is as a teacher, and he only does corporate negotiation as a sideline. So he's not likely to be able to implement an organizationwide process for you. Both ACME and Think! are full-time, "purpose-built" negotiation firms—it's all we do.

As far as ACME is concerned, you told me, and I agree, that your business is unique and requires a high degree of customization. ACME does provide a good quality training experience, but they don't write case studies for participant practice that are customized to your industry, and they don't spend a lot of time showing how to apply the concepts to live negotiation. Also, ACME provides salespeople with 137 tactics and countermeasures, which makes for an interesting class but can't really be implemented as an organizationwide process.

You should have noticed two things about this example. The first is that our presentation of the Gap (the difference between us and the customer's CNA) was based on what we know about the customer's needs in this particular deal, the competition, and our own value proposition. The second thing you should have noticed is that although we did show the customer how we would meet their needs better than our competition, we did it in a diplomatic way that enabled the customer to make an informed decision, one based on elements of their CNA.

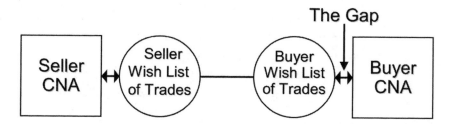

You should note, though, that it's never a good idea to attempt to communicate such a direct CNA Gap analysis unless you're at least reasonably confident of what you know about the customer's CNA and needs in this negotiation. If you present what you think makes you better when you don't really know their needs, or misdiagnose a Gap in the competition's value proposition given the customer's needs, it will come back to bite you.

But what happens after you've presented your MEOs? Well, every once in a very rare while your customer may simply accept one of them as presented. You shouldn't count on it, though. What's much more likely to happen is that your customer will start looking for ways to change the terms of one or more of the MEOs. And that's when the trading starts. In the meantime, though, because you'll have anchored the negotiation and diplomatically educated the customer on how your offer is better than their CNA, you'll have established an advantageous starting point for the discussion.

BASIC TRADING SKILLS

The four-step process for blueprinting negotiations is easy to remember, even if only because all it basically does is answer these two questions: "What are the consequences if we do not reach agreement?" and "What items are likely to be included if we do reach agreement?" At the same time, what Eric Fellman says about life in his book *The Power Behind Positive Thinking* (HarperCollins, 1997) can also be said of the process: "It's simple, it's just not easy." In fact, in that respect our process avoids the failings of most negotiation training, which usually offers long lists of tactics and countertactics that are not only difficult to remember but may not mesh with your personal style as a negotiator. I don't feel it's either necessary or, for the matter, even advisable to tell you exactly what words to use for two good reasons. First, you probably wouldn't be able to remember them, and, second, even if you could, there's no reason why you shouldn't use your own words.

A Rational Way of Responding to Tactics

It's in this spirit that I'd like to offer you a process for responding to the other side's tactics. Throughout the book I've shown you how to uncover and anticipate those tactics, but this skill—which improves with time—can be extremely helpful during the trading-tactical phase of a negotiation. The three steps of the process are:

1. Determine whether the tactic is unrealistic anchor related, single-issue trade related, or misdiagnosed CNA related.
2. Restate the tactic in terms of the Strategic Negotiation Process.
3. Use the skills of the process to respond appropriately.

These steps are based on the premise that virtually every tactic that comes from the other side can be traced back to anchors, trades, or CNA. Following are some examples to help you recognize the kinds of tactics you're likely to encounter. (And remember they're just examples and absolutely not meant to be memorized!)

Common Anchoring Tactics

- "My budget is X."
- "Last year's price was X."
- "I expect an X percent reduction off last year's price."

Common CNA Tactics

- "Your competition is lower."
- "I can get the same thing better, faster, and cheaper."
- "As a supplier, you're the most inflexible and difficult to deal with."

Common Trading Tactics

- "You need to sharpen your pencil."
- "Can you throw that in for free?"
- "Give me a break on that item."

Once you've figured out where any particular tactic is coming from, the next step is to put it into the language of the process. In our workshops, for example, when a participant tells a story that ends with something like ". . . anyway, after all that the customer had the audacity to tell me I had to sharpen my pencil," we respond with "So you're telling me the customer asked for a one-item concession." Thinking through the tactic in this way, and categorizing it, enables you to be more objective and, as a result, less emotional in dealing with it.

Of course, identifying the tactic and restating it so you can see it more objectively are important, but the next step—responding—is even more so. How do you do that? The best way of responding to an anchoring tactic is to simply ignore it. By ignore it I don't mean that you pretend your customer didn't say anything. What I mean is that you acknowledge hearing what they've said and then ask a question or two about other elements of the negotiation to get them off the subject.

The one thing you should never do when responding to an anchoring tactic is to reanchor the negotiation. Let's say, for example, that there's a very high demand for your Gizmo (your CNA); you're selling it for an average price of $29.95; and your customer tries to anchor the price at $11.00. If you respond by saying, "You're crazy, I get at least $29.95 for my Gizmo," what you've done is created an Agreement Zone that looks like this:

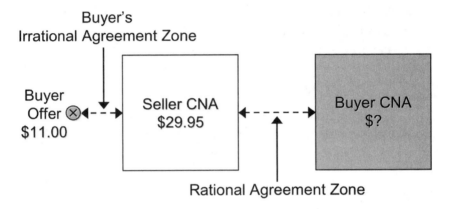

Because, on average, a deal like this will close somewhere around the middle of the Agreement Zone, or at about $20.00, if you reanchor at $29.95, you'll wind up with nearly $10.00 less than your average market selling price. So, again, the best way to respond is by ignoring it and moving on.

When a customer uses a trading tactic, all you have to do is remember the two rules I mentioned earlier: "Never concede—always trade" and "Never negotiate one thing by itself." Even though, again, I can't absolutely guarantee that this way of responding to tactics will work every time, doing it this way will substantially increase your chances of closing successfully.

Finally, so far as CNA tactics are concerned, there are two ways of responding depending on the situation. If the client actually does have a better, faster, and/or cheaper value proposition as his Consequence of No Agreement, you should adjust your offer accordingly. On the other hand, if the client is bluffing or is mistaken about their CNA, the best course to follow is to diplomatically educate them by providing a rational analysis of the difference between the various alternatives.

Here are some examples of the frequently encountered tactics mentioned above, how they can be evaluated, and how you might respond to them. Again, I'm not suggesting that you use these particular words. These examples are provided just to give you an idea of what I'm talking about.

Buyer Tactic: "My budget is X."
Evaluation: This is an anchor-related tactic, and it has nothing to do with your pricing.
Response: "I understand your concern about your budget, but how do the volume and length of contract issues we discussed compare in importance to pricing?"

Buyer Tactic: "You need to sharpen your pencil."
Evaluation: This is a trading-related tactic in which your customer is trying to force you into a one-item concession
Response: "I'd be happy to build an offer with a lower price. Can we talk about lengthening the contract or adding in one more product line?"

Buyer Tactic: "Your competition is lower."
Evaluation: This is a CNA-related tactic in which the customer is saying that his CNA is better than your offer.
Response: "My competitor may be cheaper when you look at just the domestic element of the offer, but does it still look the same when you factor in the international element?"

Again, after looking at literally hundreds of tactics, we've found that virtually all of them fall into one of these three areas. And if you go back to what you know about anchoring, Wish Lists, and CNA, you'll find that responding this way is quite easy and effective. You will also find that your response will be based on facts and analysis rather than on emotions.

Diagnose: Anchor
Rational response: Ignore by asking questions

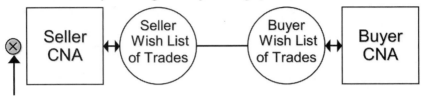

Irrational Anchor

Diagnose: CNA tactic
Rational response: Diplomatically educate

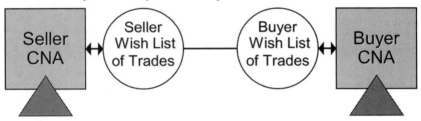

Diagnose: Trade tactic
Rational response: Always trade, never concede

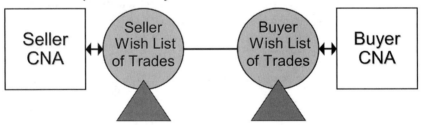

Let's do a quick test. Your customer says, "I'm overpaying compared to what you charge other customers in the market." Is this primarily:

a. An unrealistic anchor?
b. A single-item concession request?
c. A misdiagnosed CNA?

The answer is (c) A misdiagnosed CNA. The client has assumed—incorrectly—that if you don't reach agreement with him or her, you'll sell your product to someone else at a lower price. The most appropriate way to respond to this would be to say something like: "Actually, that's not true. Some of our customers do have lower prices, but we're either not doing warehousing for them, which you said you wanted, or their volume is at least three times the size of what we're talking about here." In any case, as you can see, dividing all possible tactics into only three categories makes them much more manageable and much easier to respond to.

The Customer's Ideal MEO

When the trading begins, one of the first things a customer is likely to ask for is the most complete MEO—the most expensive—at the price of the least complete—the least expensive. Lots of people have been taught that it never hurts to ask—which is usually true—so they figure the worst thing you can do is say no. Of course, that's exactly what you should say. A very diplomatic way to say no without actually saying it is to say something like "Sure, we can find you a lower-priced option. We just need to adjust the offering a bit based on your needs." Then you can move items in and out of the MEOs and rearrange the pricing until you've found a way that will satisfy both sides.

To do that it's often helpful to ask the customer to rank the MEOs from one to three in order of their most to least desirable. Doing so accomplishes several purposes. First, you're not asking for any commitment, so the customer doesn't have to be defensive, but at the same time you are working together. Second, if there are multiple buying influences in the room, you can learn a lot from what they say among themselves as they discuss how to rank the offers. I was once in a meeting in which the seller was offering three MEOs for some factory automation software. When the buyer said he'd rank the lowest-priced offer the highest, the vice president of manufacturing literally jumped out of her chair and said, "I don't care how little we pay for it; if it doesn't work on the plant floor, we've paid too much for it." The group quickly reranked the offers, and the option with lots of service and support moved up a notch. The third advantage of having your customer rank the MEOs is that, on the basis of the final ranking, you can determine what is most to least important to the customers. If, for example, they rank as lowest the option that has 24/7 support, and they rank as highest the one that guarantees install time, you get even more detail on their prioritized Wish List.

Repricing the Offer

Once you have a clear picture of your customer's ideal MEO, you will probably need to reprice that offer. I strongly suggest that you do this separately from the group, either in a five-minute break or when you come back the next day. The reason for this is that the prices of MEOs are essentially based on the prices of their individual items, so if you have to recalculate the price, it's easier—and better—for you to do it without your customer sitting there waiting. I also suggest that, to the greatest extent possible, you suggest a price for the entire package rather than for each individual item. If you price the items separately, your customer will probably ask for cost reductions on each one. And remember that you never want to negotiate any one item by itself.

You can, if necessary, break down the package into several component parts and suggest a price for each. For example, if you have nine or ten items in an MEO for a customer who's pushing you on line-item pricing, you might be able to break all the items into three categories— such as design of the solution, delivery of the solution, and ongoing maintenance—and provide prices for each. Doing so can help you avoid even being put into a situation in which you can be asked to negotiate on one item.

Let's say, for example, that you've made a very low-priced offer in which you've done everything you can to trade risk back to the customer, including eliminating free service that detracts from your own profits. Now, though, the customer comes to you and asks that you put the service back in because your competitor offers free service. How do you counter such a request? It's difficult, to say the least. For one thing, you don't know all the variables of the deal your competitor offered. They may, for example, be offering free service but at a much higher overall price and/or with larger volume commitments. Because of that, unless your customer is willing to show you everything that your competitor has offered, which is certainly not likely to happen, you can't do an "apples-to-apples" comparison. It may be, too, that your product or service is simply better than your competitor's (the customer's CNA) and you don't offer free service because it's rarely needed. The point here is that it's best if you can avoid being put into this kind of situation in the first place.

One of our selling clients dealt with this type of situation in a very interesting way. They were selling software to one of the largest chip manufacturers in the world, and the customer kept going back to the MEO and asking for concessions on individual aspects of the multiple trades that were part of the offer. Our client tried to explain that the entire deal was a package, but the customer just didn't seem to understand. After several fruitless attempts at explaining, the seller finally said, "Look, I'm trying to achieve X percent gross margin here. I'm willing to move on as many items as you want, but you have to understand that if I do, I'll have to adjust something else to achieve that margin." That got through to the buyer, and they then proceeded to work together to devise trades that the buyer was comfortable with and, at the same time, provided the seller with the gross margin they were looking for.

Responding to Outrageous Demands

Finally, it's important for you to bear in mind that just because a customer asks for something doesn't mean you have to respond. Buyers sometimes make truly outrageous demands, but that's no reason for you to go back to headquarters to ask for whatever it is they're demanding. The important thing to remember, regardless of how outrageous the request may be, is to not get emotional about it. What you should do, instead, is simply ask for a trade in return. Eventually, your customer will begin to understand that trading is good for both sides, and that they're likely to get more of what they want if they're willing to trade with you. The number of margin-reducing concessions two people can make may be small, but the number of value-creating trades they can make is limited only by time and their creativity.

• • • • •

So now you've constructed three custom MEOs, presented overviews of them to your customer, provided details on each, had the customer rank them in order of preference, traded some items in and out of the highest-ranked MEO, and changed the pricing a bit. What you've done here, whether you realize it or not, is *create and divide value*. Trading, which is the cooperative aspect of the process, is what enabled you to create value by essentially putting more money into the deal. And claiming that value, which is the competitive aspect, is what enabled you to divide that money. More often than not, by the time a deal is closed, the buyers have won a few and the sellers have won a few. But the important point here is that by using the Strategic Negotiation Process to blueprint negotiations, both sides come out of the deal better than they anticipated when they went into it. They've not only achieved a "win-win" situation; they've gone beyond it.

My experience suggests that there are essentially three types of negotiators. The first is the "tough" negotiator, the type who closes a large percentage of his or her deals, but the deals tend to be small because they leave value-creating trades on the table. The second type is the "nice" or "easy" negotiator, the type who tends to trade well and close a lot of deals but gives up too much of the joint value to the other side. The third type is what I call the "rational" negotiator, and that's what you should be. This is the type who is strong in the cooperative aspect that will increase the likelihood of closure and creating true value but is also strong in the competitive aspect, claiming as much value as possible without hurting the relationship.

This raises the question of what's "fair" in terms of dividing the pie. Many people think of 50-50 as fair. Although there's a certain logic to that, the problem with it is that you're usually splitting 50-50 of a completely arbitrary number! Let's say that what you're selling has a market value of $100; the customer offers an arbitrary $50 and then says, "Let's split the difference and agree on $75." It's certainly a very easy way to settle a deal, but there's nothing particularly fair about it. Nor, obviously, is it something you'd want to do.

You've achieved fairness in a negotiation any time you can claim as much of the created joint value as possible without forcing the other side to take a deal that's worse than their CNA. Leaving your customer with something less than their CNA is what I call "hosing" the other side, and it's typically neither a good thing to do in ongoing relationships nor a good message to send to the market. As I mentioned earlier, what you want to do is claim as much of that zone as possible by anchoring only marginally better than the other side's CNA. If you anchor far better than the other side's CNA to be "fair," you'll be giving up too much value. And if you anchor marginally better than your own CNA, you're likely to leave money on the table. But if you anchor marginally better than the other side's CNA, you'll be able to claim most of the value and still give the other side a win by exceeding their CNA plus the extra value you created by trading.

ADVANCED TRADING SKILLS

You now have all the tools you need to conduct successful, value-creating negotiations in the majority of situations you're likely to encounter. There are, however, a few additional tools that it would be advantageous to have for those rare occasions when you may need them. These tools—or *advanced skills*—will cover the roughly one out of five situations that you haven't already prepared for.

Postsettlement Settlements

You may, on occasion, find yourself in a situation in which you've closed a particularly tough deal but, even though you have reached agreement, still feel that both sides may have left some money on the table, and that it could hurt the relationship. In that kind of situation you might want to suggest to your customer what we call a postsettlement settlement. This is an opportunity to come to the table one last time in an effort to make the deal better. If you choose to do so, though, you should go into the meeting with the understanding that if both sides don't agree to a new deal, the old one stands. This usually works quite well and often results in a better deal for both sides. Part of the reason for this, I suspect, is that there's something liberating about going back to the table with an already existing deal as both sides' CNA, which makes it possible to craft an even better one.

"Parachute Items"—The Fourth MEO

In anticipation of a difficult negotiation or as the result of one, you might want to devise a fourth Multiple Equal Offer. Rather than offer it up front, though, you hold it back to use as a parachute if all else seems to be failing and it looks as if you're not going to be able to make a deal. If you choose this option, you should make sure that the fourth MEO includes some creative trades, particularly items that aren't officially on the table, as out-of-the-box trades are often the ones that prompt people to think creatively on both sides. In fact, it's frequently MEOs like these that allow you to break through impasses, as was the case with the insurance company and the home improvement retailer I mentioned earlier. Doing this can be particularly satisfying, because when it works it's like having a really great deal emerge from the ashes!

Contingent Contracts, or "Bets"

It's not uncommon for both sides to come to the table with lots of biased data that they use to confirm their vision of the future. Depending on the situation, this may not be a problem. But negotiating over something that may or may not happen in the future can—and sometimes does—lead to impasse. We've found that when you're negotiating over something like this—such as the price or availability of a new product, volume, or service—a good way of dealing with it, rather than simply arguing, is to "bet" on your version of the outcome. That is, you suggest to those on the other side that you include something in the agreement that says "If this occurs, I pay X, and if that occurs, you pay Y." These contingent contracts, or "bets," aren't only great tools for overcoming impasse but can also be used if the other side is bluffing, because if they are, they won't be willing to "put their money where their mouth is."

Define/Correct Impasse

There are essentially only two kinds of impasses. The first, the emotional impasse, occurs when a deal is on the table that's better than both sides' CNAs, but they still don't come to an agreement. Situations like this are usually the result of one or both sides misdiagnosing their CNA. The best way to deal with this is to go back and evaluate the CNAs again, validate them again, diplomatically educate the other side about them, and re-present the offer.

The second kind of impasse is the structural impasse, which occurs when the deal on the table isn't as good as the CNA of one or both sides, and as a result they can't come to agreement. Let's say, for example, that a deal is on the table, but the two sides are $2,000 apart based on their CNAs—the buyer can get it cheaper (for $4,000), and the seller can get a higher price ($6,000). There are two options in this situation. The first is to simply walk away from the deal, and sometimes that makes sense; after all, not all deals should happen. In fact, many times walking away from a deal below market yield makes more money for you in the long run, because you don't reset your price in the market. (A steel manufacturer customer of ours says that 5 tons of discounted steel can result in 500 tons of discounted steel.) If, however, it's a deal that should happen, the best way to correct this kind of structural impasse is to attempt to find other items to trade into the deal that create an additional $2,000 of value that can be used to close the Gap. This might include something like incremental business in another division or the client's picking up a new product line.

Underlying Interest: Risk/Reward

Sometimes, no matter what kind of trade you suggest during this stage of the negotiation, you still feel as though you're running into a brick wall. Your customer is insisting on something that you just can't give in on, and there doesn't seem to be any way out. An excellent way, however, that lets you avoid impasse in a situation like this does exist. That way is for you to ask a series of questions designed to help you understand why your customer is being so insistent: "Help me understand why that's important." "How does that have an impact on your personal success?" "How does it have an impact on your department's success?" "Why is that so high on your priority list?" In asking such questions, you will in all likelihood discover a substantial difference between *what* your customer is asking for and *why* he or she is asking for it.

Let's look at length of contract as an example. Normally, you would want a contract to run as long as possible in order to lower your company's risk and ensure longer-term cash flow. Your customer, on the other hand, will probably want to keep the length as short as possible to have the flexibility of taking advantage of new and emerging suppliers. In a situation like this, you can argue two versus three years until you're both blue in the face, but it's only by understanding the underlying interests involved that you'll be able to find a way to address them and reach agreement. In fact, once you've found out why someone wants something, you can usually find several different ways to fill that need. For example, in situations like this one I've often seen deals that include a right-of-first-refusal clause that speaks to the underlying interests of those on both sides of the table. In fact, underlying interest is one of the key aspects of trading in negotiations, particularly in legal and personal negotiation and to a lesser degree in business-to-business negotiation. It is, however, a very useful skill and one that's taught in most sales courses and basic negotiation texts.

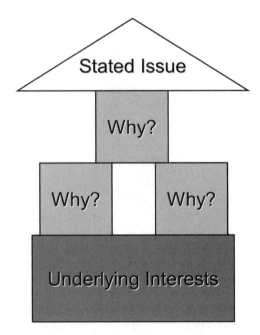

Closing: Hesitation

Finally, you've probably run into situations in which a deal is virtually done, but for some reason your customer is hesitating about finalizing it. Assuming that you've attained your initial goal to "create joint

DEALING WITH *Professional* **Buyers**

In developing and presenting MEOs for a professional buyer, it's extremely important to use what you've learned during the sales process and the validation step to address the concerns of the buyer's internal customers. This means that you have to make sure that your MEOs exploit the Gap between what you have to offer and what the buyer and his or her customers consider their Consequences of No Agreement. It also means that you must embed trades into your offers not only from the buyer's Wish List but also from those of his or her customers.

Ideally, you will have the opportunity to present your MEOs to both the buyer and his or her internal customers. If you're not able to, however, you must be sure to point out to the buyer those trades that you included to satisfy the concerns of others in his or her organization. In the end, not only will both of you have a deal that goes beyond "win-win," you'll also have established the kind of mutually beneficial relationship that can continue indefinitely into the future.

value and divide it given concerns for fairness in the ongoing relationship," the chances are that your customer's hesitation is based on a lack of understanding of their CNA, a misdiagnosis of it, or a feeling that a better offer is still out there. In this kind of situation, the best way to get that slow closer to move is to go back to your CNA Gap analysis and remind your customer of how what you have to offer is better than what he or she can get from going to one of your competitors, doing it themselves, or doing nothing at all.

Best **P**ractices **R**eview

- Overview each MEO before going into detail.
- Don't expect offers to be accepted right away; ask to have them ranked.
- Be prepared to trade.
- Be prepared to demonstrate the CNA Gap.
- Use an analytical approach to respond to tactics (i.e, diagnose tactics as anchor related, trading related, or CNA related, and respond rationally based on your knowledge of the blueprint.

Common Mistakes to Avoid

- Losing sight of your goal of creating joint value in the face of irrational pressure from the other side.
- Using emotion rather than diagnosis as a response to tactics.
- Agreeing to items one at a time; nothing is agreed on until everything's agreed on.

. . . . .

You have now completed all four steps of our process for blueprinting negotiations in that you have done the following:

- Developed a goal to "create joint value and divide it given concerns for fairness in the ongoing relationship"
- Conducted Consequences of No Agreement and Trading Estimations for both sides in the negotiation
- Validated those estimations by using public sources, asking questions of colleagues, and soliciting information from your customer
- Used all the information you've gathered to prepare the offers you will make
- Presented the offers, traded with your customer, and finalized the deal

Now that you have been through the entire process, you've no doubt realized that it's based on watching thousands of people negotiate, learning the habits of the most successful, and recognizing the most common mistakes of those who are less successful. You should also have realized that the process is quite intuitive, and that to a great extent it's based on what you already do. The only differences are that now you see it as part of a process and you can now do it at a new, world-class level of professionalism.

To help you put all you've learned together, in the next chapter I show you how to blueprint two deals from start to finish—one ad hoc negotiation with an existing customer and one larger and more strategic deal with a new customer—as well as a special bonus example showing how the Strategic Negotiation Process can be applied to any kind of negotiation.

APPLYING
THE PROCESS

Chapter

11

PUTTING IT
ALL TOGETHER

Sample Negotiations

Congratulations! You now have all
the tools you need to become a world-class, cutting-edge negotiator. As
you begin to put those tools to use, you'll find that using the Strategic
Negotiation Process to blueprint business deals is not only an amazingly
effective means of attaining success in negotiations but also an extremely
efficient one. It may not seem like it at the moment, but, if so, that's only
because the process is still new to you. The more you use the process, the
more practice you get and the easier and more effective it will become.

Just to make sure, though, that each step of the blueprinting process
is clear to you, and to give you a little additional practice before you go
out into the real world, in this chapter I show you how to blueprint two
sample negotiations. The first is an ad hoc negotiation with an existing
customer, and the second is a large and more strategic negotiation with
a new customer. And to show you that our process can be used for any
kind of negotiation, as an added bonus I show you at the end how to
blueprint an entirely different kind of negotiation.

SAMPLE ONE: USING THE BLUEPRINTING PROCESS IN A SMALL AD HOC NEGOTIATION

It's Tuesday afternoon, you just got back from lunch, and you find you have a voice mail message from one of your customers. You closed a deal with them about six months ago—agreeing on price, terms, service, volume, and length of contact—and the deal's due to be renegotiated six months from now. But in his message the customer says that he's being pushed hard by management to reduce costs and he wants an additional 5 percent off the price. He also says that he needs an answer from you for a three o'clock meeting with his boss, which means you've got two hours to blueprint this negotiation.

Establishing a Negotiation Goal (Five Minutes)

The first thing you do is remember that your goal in any negotiation is to "create joint value and divide it given concerns for fairness in the ongoing relationship." What that means more specifically in this situation is that, despite the fact that your customer is demanding a zero-sum concession, you want to find a way to create joint value without hurting the relationship you created when you made the original deal.

Estimating the Blueprint: The CNA Estimation (Ten Minutes)

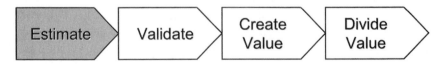

Your side (five minutes). First, you complete a quick overview of your own CNA. You recognize that if you don't reach agreement with your customer on this, there's a very good chance that he'll get emotional and try to get out of the contract. Your CNA, then, is to lose the business. In this case, losing the business means losing about $75,000 in revenue you've forecast for this customer in the short term, the remaining six months of the contract. But because you'd also like to renew the contract for another year, losing the business means a potential loss of another $75,000 to $100,000, for a total CNA cost of up to $175,000.

On the other hand, a contract is a contract, and there may be some benefit in not giving in to their demand and sending the message that they can't continue to do this to you. At the same time you know that if you have to take legal action against them to enforce the contract, there will probably be some hard legal costs associated with it, some soft costs in the form of the hassles associated with suing a customer, and, of course, the hard costs of losing the customer once the contract expires.

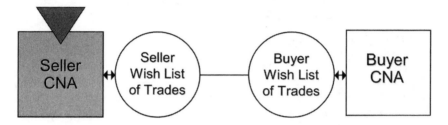

Their side (five minutes). You estimate that they will either keep the agreement "as is" or try to switch to your nearest competitor, Operations Consulting. Knowing the emotional volatility of this customer, you guess that their most likely CNA is to try to dump you and take their business to the competition.

Going to your competitor would be of some benefit to your customer because Operations Consulting is much smaller than your company and your customer would accordingly be a bigger fish in a smaller pond there. In addition, Operations Consulting would probably offer your customer lower fees—at least in the short term—to attract them over. On the other hand, Operations Consulting doesn't have global offices as you do, which means the customer will have to sign up subcontractors in several sites around the world to handle their consulting

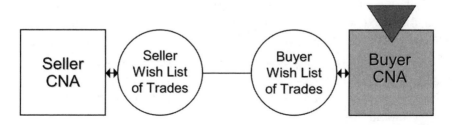

needs. This represents a lot of risk for your customer as well as the hassle of finding, signing up, and starting the learning curve with several new firms. In addition, they have to start all over domestically with Operations Consulting if they kick you out.

Power analysis. On the basis of your CNA Estimation, you think that you have slightly more power in the negotiation than your customer does because of the Gap between their needs (a global solution) and their CNA, which is a domestic firm, and the fact that you already have a contract with them.

Estimating the Blueprint: The Wish List Estimation (Five Minutes)

Your side. Certainly, lowering your price would be the last item on your Wish List. But as you sit at your desk and look at your sales plan for the account, you come up with a few items that you would readily trade in exchange for the price discounts:

- Agreeing to another year now instead of six months from now
- Access to a division of your customer's business that you don't have today
- Selling them your new operations management software

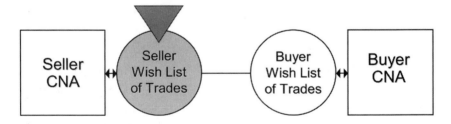

Their side. Even though this customer is quite pushy, you know that they like working with you because you've had a positive impact on their operations. You also know that although their lead issue is price, they are actually concerned about several things at the moment:

- A discount of an additional 5 percent, and you doubt if you'll get them lower

- A possible interest in your new software, which will be just a simple yes or no for 100 licenses
- The ease and low cost of introducing you to their other divisions, and, depending on the value of a discount, there's a range of two to three divisions you'd like to get into
- A possible willingness to extend the contract, and you think a range of 6 to 12 months is possible

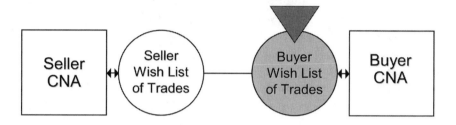

Validating the Estimation (20 Minutes)

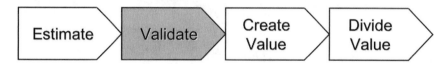

Based on your estimation, you prepare some quick questions, then call the customer, and say:

- "Bob, I understand your company is under profit pressure, and you'd like us to help you achieve your goal of a 5 percent cost reduction. Is that right? I may have some creative ideas for how we can get there, but I need some help brainstorming for a few minutes. Can I run a few questions by you?"
- "Have you received the direct mail piece announcing our new operations management software? How did you feel about it?"
- "I'd very much like to gain access to your Latin American Division. How are your contacts there?"
- "We're about six months into our contract now. How happy are you with us overall?"
- "Do you think that at the end of this contract we'll be asked to bid on your business again?"

- "I've heard that Operations Consulting has been pushing you hard to bring your business to them. Is that right?"
- "They're small, and I'm sure they'd love to have you as a customer. Have they added global operations yet?"
- "Great! I really appreciate your time. I'm going to e-mail you some ideas for your consideration, and then I'll call you back in about half an hour. My goal is to come up with a way to get you your discount and keep our end of the deal as valuable to us as it is today. We really value your business, and I don't want to do anything to lose it and have to find a new customer. I also don't want you to have to go through the hassle of replacing us."

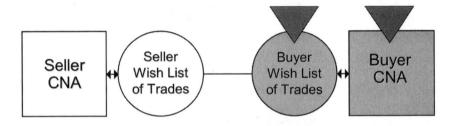

Using the Blueprint to Create Value (15 Minutes)

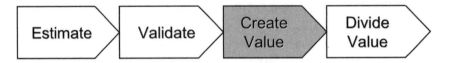

As soon as possible after you get off the phone with Bob, you prepare an e-mail to him that says the following:

Dear Bob,

Thanks for agreeing to our earlier phone call. It helped me go a long way toward fulfilling your request. As you'll see below, I have several ideas that are intended to increase the value of our relationship for both of us. I'll phone you shortly, and I hope we'll be able to agree on one that you can present at your three o'clock meeting.

Item	Option 1: Existing Relationship with New Added Value	Option 2: Broader Relationship	Option 3: Longer and Broader
Price Discount	3%	5%	8%
New Software	100 licenses @ $29.95	100 licenses @ $29.95	100 Licenses @ $29.95
Introduction to Mgt. at Latin American Division	_____	Yes, with reference	Yes, with reference
Contract Length	_____	_____	Agree to 12-month extension now

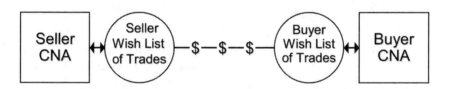

Using the Blueprint to Divide Value (15 Minutes)

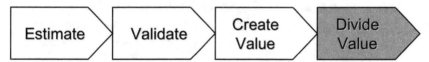

When you call Bob to follow up on your e-mail, he tells you that the first offer doesn't meet their needs, so you agree to cross that one off. He is, however, very much interested in the possibility of being able to bring not only a 5 percent discount but an 8 percent discount to his three o'clock meeting. He tells you that he'll look like a star in front of all the other buyers if he can pull that off. So you do a little trading and finalize this deal:

FINAL AGREEMENT
Price Discount: 7 percent
New Software: 100 licenses @ $25 per person
Introduction to Management at the Latin American Division: Yes, with reference
Contract Length: Agree to a six-month extension now

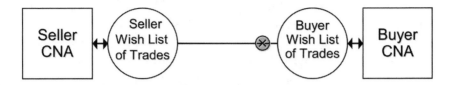

This example should give you a pretty clear idea of exactly how effective and efficient blueprinting a small, ad hoc negotiation can be. You started with a difficult situation—a customer asking for a zero-sum concession—and even though you did give some on price, what you got in return was sales of a new product, an introduction to another division of your customer's company, and a six-month extension of your contract. Not bad for a little more than an hour's work!

Again, as you can see, you started off by estimating your CNA and Wish List as well as those of your customer. Then, in a validation phone call you were able to confirm your estimates, let your customer know that you'd thought through his likely CNA and its effects, and subtly anchor on multiple issues. You then presented three Multiple Equal Offers, ignoring the single-item anchor of a 5 percent price reduction, and you used the opportunity to offer them more than they wanted in exchange for more than you thought you could get. And with a little trading you created and divided value in a way that enabled you not only to go beyond "win-win" but to further solidify your relationship with the customer.

Let's now look at how you might blueprint a negotiation on a multi-million-dollar new global account with a team of sellers on your side and a team of sellers on the buyer's side.

SAMPLE TWO: USING THE BLUEPRINTING PROCESS IN A LARGE AND COMPLEX NEGOTIATION

It's April 1 and you've just been told by a potential new global customer that after all your months of trying to sell some of your machines to them, it's finally down to a choice between you and your closest competitor. The customer wants to see your "best foot forward" proposal in six weeks (by May 15) and has hinted that your competitor is aggressively pursuing them, is being quite creative on price, and has a pretty good product fit.

Establishing a Negotiation Goal (Five Minutes)

As always, the first thing you must do in beginning this negotiation is to remember that your goal is to "create joint value and divide it given concerns for fairness in the ongoing relationship."

Estimating the Blueprint: The CNA Estimation (Two-and-a-Half to Three Hours)

Your side (30 minutes). You complete a quick overview of your own CNA and determine that you will most likely lose the business if you don't reach agreement with the customer in this negotiation. In this case, losing the business means that based on your short-term forecast for this customer, you will lose about $750,000 in global revenue in the first year. If, however, you take into consideration potential long-term revenues from this customer, total CNA costs could be as much as $2.5 million. In addition, by not closing this deal you will lose the costs associated with the four months you've spent selling to the customer—approximately $25,000 for staff time, product demonstrations, and so on.

You will also have some soft costs in the form of "political heat" from your vice president of global sales and the head of your product management group, both of whom have taken a personal interest in this sale as it affects their bonuses as well as yours. In addition, losing this sale will, in effect, fund a competitor by sending these revenues to them.

The only good news here is that the market is growing, albeit slowly compared to past years, the chances of replacing this customer are fairly good, and your list of other prospects for sales looks good at the moment. Also, while you have no other customers that are this large and ready to close, there are at least two or three smaller ones that you feel positive about. All of them together could replace this sale, but it's always more profitable to close and service one customer than several.

Their side (two to three hours). As always, attempting to analyze the customer's CNA is a bit trickier. In this case, you know their CNA is to go to your major competitor and, or so they've hinted, for less money. What's tricky, though, is the total analysis—that is, determining the positive and negative effects—of choosing the competitor over you. The first thing you do is pull together a team from your side. You invite one of your company's account managers, who once worked for your competitor on this deal, a guy from engineering who just came to you from the customer's organization, and some additional product experts. You give them an overview of the situation and ask them to help you brainstorm all the "elements" the customer should be considering when comparing your offer with their CNA.

After brainstorming the elements, you go back and ask the group whether, from the customer's perspective, these elements are positives or negatives compared to choosing you. The team breaks down the analysis in terms of design of the solution, delivery and installation, ongoing maintenance, output, and long-term upkeep. The team members also suggest doing an evaluation of comparative terms and conditions. The results of their analysis suggest the questions that must be addressed are:

Design Elements Questions

- Is there an off-the-shelf solution that fits the customer's needs?
- How much "ground up" design is needed to build and test custom aspects?
- How much time/commitment is needed from the customer for design?

Delivery and Installation Elements Questions

- How long will it take?
- How long will the customer's operation be down while the machine is being installed?
- How labor intensive will it be for the customer?

Maintenance Elements Questions

- How often does the machine break down?
- What are the service hours and fees?
- How difficult would it be to train the customer's team to run it?

Output Elements Questions

- How many units per hour will their machine put out?
- What is the defect rate of the customer's machine?
- Can they run 24/7?

Upkeep Elements Questions

- What do maintenance costs look like in years two, three, and four?
- How easily upgradable is the machine?
- What is the machine's expected life?

Terms and Conditions Elements Questions

- Is it better to lease or buy?
- How much flexibility is there in contracting?
- What are the payment terms?
- What is the short-term product price?

Now, you've determined in regard to design that your competitor does have a pretty good off-the-shelf machine, and yours would require some customization. Your customization, however, would be free and would require very little customer interface.

As for installation, your engineering department has just found some independent studies showing that machines that are easily customized—like yours—are also relatively easy to install, and therefore end up taking about as much time to put in as less flexible off-the-shelf machines.

As far as maintenance is concerned, the folks in your engineering department, especially the engineer that just came over from the customer, say that you have a huge advantage in terms of your machine's reliability. Of course, customers aren't likely to tell you that, but it's one of your strengths.

In regard to output, you and your customer are pretty close. Their output may be a bit higher than yours, but your machines run a higher percentage of the time and thus probably make up for the difference.

In terms of upkeep, your machines break down much less frequently and as a result last longer because of how they've been engineered.

Finally, in regard to terms and conditions, you and your competitor both offer lease or buy options, your industry contracts are all pretty much the same, and payment terms are usually 25 percent at signing, 25 percent on delivery, and 50 percent when running. Your "price" is a bit higher, but you've determined that because of the reliability and flexibility of your machines, they have less downtime, easier long-term upgrades, and longer shelf life. As a result, not only does your return on investment (ROI) get better after year one but your product is less expensive to own in years two and three.

Power analysis. In answering the questions about each group of elements, you've determined that there is a Gap between what you have to offer and the customer's CNA (your competitor) in all but one of them (output). Based on that, you feel that you should have more power in this negotiation. The only problem is that either your customer doesn't have all the data on their CNA that you do or they're bluffing.

Estimating the Blueprint: The Wish List Estimation (Two Hours)

Your side (30 minutes). You've pulled together your product manager, pricing manager, and someone from the legal department for this estimation and, after much wrangling, have prioritized your Wish List of trades as follows:

	Wish List Estimation		
	Our Side		
Rank	*Item*	*Weight*	*Range (High to Low)*
1.	Length of contract	30%	3 to 1 years
2.	Price	25%	$300 to $250,000 per machine
3.	Volume	15%	3 to 2 machines
4.	Upgrades	15%	50% discount to free
5.	Man hours provided by you to install	10%	100 to 150
6.	Ongoing service	5%	8/5 to 24/7

Their side (one-and-a-half hours). With the help of the account manager who used to work for your competitor and your pricing manager, you've estimated the types of trades this customer has looked for in the past and come up with the following educated guesses for their Wish List:

Wish List Estimation

The Other Side

Rank	Item	Weight	Range (High to Low)
1.	Price	40%	$200 to $300,000 per machine
2.	Ongoing service	25%	24/7 to 8/5
3.	Upgrades	15%	Free to 75% discount
4.	Length of contract	10%	1 year to ???
5.	Volume	5%	2 machines to ???
6.	Man hours provided by you to install	5%	200 to 100

Validating the Estimation (One Day)

Validating the CNA Estimation. You know exactly what the customer's CNA is, and you've done a pretty good job of analyzing its positive and negative elements. Now, in order to learn how your customer sees their CNA and to educate them about it, you prepare the following questions:

- Have you determined how much customization the two machines will need to install?
- How do you see the impact on your facility during installation?
- Do you have a certain amount of time budgeted for installation?
- What are your expectations in terms of machine downtime?
- When the machine breaks down, how quickly do you expect service?
- How much staff retraining do you expect you'll need?
- Do you have a figure in mind for year-one maintenance costs?
- Do you have figures in mind for costs in years two through four?
- How would you like to handle future upgrades?
- Do you complete total cost of ownership analyses or just compare acquisition price?

Validating the Wish List Estimation. Having developed questions to validate your customer's CNA, you now develop questions to validate their Wish List items as follows:

- I understand you will be looking to negotiate price, service, up-grades, length of contract, volume, and man hours to install. Is that right? Is there anything missing? Is there anything that should be deleted?
- What would you rank as your lead priority? That is, what should we focus on most? How about second, third, fourth, and so on?
- Do you have any specific targets you'd like to hit for each item?

You now send out an e-mail to the head buyer, vice president of manufacturing, vice president of finance, and all the other people you've been selling to, and ask them if you can have 15 minutes of their time to better understand their needs for the upcoming negotiation. If they ask for them, you can send the questions in advance. When you get together with them, whether on the phone or in person, you ask the easy Wish List questions first to get the ball rolling and then go on to the CNA questions. You also bring someone else from your account team with you to record the customer's answers.

Using the Blueprint to Create Value (One Hour)

Having had a validation meeting (or meetings) with influential managers on several levels, you now feel that even though you didn't get answers to all your questions, you were still able to tighten up your estimations. You also feel that you succeeded in educating them on many aspects of their CNA as well as on many of the items to be agreed on in the negotiation. Now, taking into account your interest in length of contract, price, and volume and theirs in price, service, and upgrades, you devise three MEOs:

Item	Option 1: Short-Term Relationship and Lower Price	Option 2: Long-Term Strategic Relationship	Option 3: A Middle Ground
Length	One year	Three years	Two years
Price	$295,000	$250,000 per machine	$275,000 per machine
Volume	One machine	Three machines	Two machines
Service	8/5	24/7	24/5

Upgrades	50% discount	Free	75% discount
Installation			
support	100 hours	300 hours	200 hours

Using the Blueprint to Divide Value (One Hour)

Now it's May 7 and you're ready to make a presentation—a full week before the customer's due date. You invite the customer's head buyer, vice president of manufacturing, and vice president of finance, and bring along product and technical support people from your side.

You open the presentation by thanking the group for taking the time to answer your questions a few weeks earlier and let them know that their doing so went a long way toward helping you customize three different potential relationships. You also tell them you realize that if they don't choose you, they will choose your nearest competitor, and you admit that your competitor has a pretty good off-the-shelf solution as well as pretty good output. You also note that during your earlier conversations the buyer and the vice president of finance put a lot of emphasis on price, and that the vice president of manufacturing talked a lot about uptime—the reliability of machines. This is the point at which you present the Gap you found in your CNA analysis, specifically:

- Your machines are higher in short-term price (year one).
- Your machines are X percent more reliable than your competitor's, resulting in:
  - Higher output (which manufacturing was concerned with).
  - Less maintenance cost (which the buyer and finance department wanted).
- The combination of higher output and lower maintenance makes your machines cost less starting late in year one and going down by X percent in years two and three.

You tell them that based on their needs and the value proposition of your competitor, you've put together three different relationships, and highlight them on a flipchart or PowerPoint presentation. You briefly overview some key elements of each, then offer everyone a handout containing the details and go through them. You now ask them to rank the three offers in terms of their preference. They quickly agree the short-term option as the least preferable, but there's a lot of internal negotiation among them over which of the remaining options is most preferable. It's obvious that neither is quite right, so at this point you begin the trading. They keep telling you that you're more expensive, but you keep going back to total costs. They try to push you for concessions, but you continue to trade. A couple of times they surprise you with demands. You quickly determine which are anchors and ignore them by asking questions or presenting more rational data, and determine which are misdiagnosed CNAs and go back to the facts of the CNA. In the end, you settle on this deal:

FINAL AGREEMENT
Length: Three years
Price: $255,000 per machine
Volume: Three machines
Service: Five days × 24 hours
Upgrades: 25% discount
Installation support: 300 hours

As you can see, both case studies—and, for that matter, virtually all negotiations—involve the basic elements of the blueprint: CNAs for both sides, Wish Lists for both sides, and a final Agreement Zone. In addition, both negotiations followed the same process for acquiring and using the data although in different time frames and by different means—phone/e-mail rather than in person. And, most important, both negotiations ended with both sides coming away with more than they had anticipated getting when they went into the negotiation.

In the Appendix, you will find two copies of a worksheet that can be used to guide the process of blueprinting business deals. The first has been completed using data from the second case study in this chapter. The second is a blank one to which you can transfer all the data you've gathered for your own negotiation so that you'll have a complete blueprint of it. The Appendix also contains some simple instructions for completing the worksheets.

• • • • •

As I said in the beginning of this chapter, the Strategic Negotiation Process doesn't only work for negotiating sales. In fact, it works—and can be applied—in literally any type of negotiation you might be involved in, even something as unlike a sales negotiation as negotiating with a child about going to bed. Look at it this way. When you're trying to get a child to bed, your immediate aim is to get him or her to go to sleep, but your ultimate goal is to do it in a way that will benefit both of you and not do any damage to your relationship. Does that sound familiar?

There are also, of course, Consequences of No Agreement for both sides. If you can't get your child to bed early (i.e., you don't reach agreement), you're going to have less time for yourself than you'd like—your CNA. The child's CNA will be that Mom and/or Dad will be annoyed with them, they won't get enough sleep, and they'll be cranky in the morning. Now, when I was a kid, my CNA was serious enough that there was no negotiation. I knew very well who had the power in any negotiation with my parents. These days, though, there's a bit more give and take.

If, however, all you do is ask them to go to bed early, it's a zero-sum concession, because for every five minutes you gain, they lose, and vice versa. So what do you do? You look for things you can trade, something of value to them that doesn't cost you very much. "Okay, son," you say, "you go to bed and I'll read you a story." As a result, your child gets something that he values highly and that costs you very little. In fact, you like it. Of course, in this case, you didn't have to do a formal estimation or validation because you already knew what was important to both of you as well as what your CNAs were. Now, if only business negotiations could be that easy. . . .

12

AN ORGANIZATIONAL APPROACH TO NEGOTIATION

In the first chapter I discussed how, in today's business environment, sellers are facing more complex negotiations, more professional buyers, more irrational competitive behavior, and more internal negotiation, all of which, of course, make negotiating more difficult. As you've now seen, however, using the Strategic Negotiation Process to blueprint individual negotiations can be enormously helpful in countering the effects of these changes. But as beneficial as using the process is for individuals, it's most effective when it's part of an organization-wide negotiation strategy. The purpose of this closing chapter, then, is to provide management with a brief overview of how companies can develop and implement such strategies.

AN ORGANIZATION-WIDE NEGOTIATION STRATEGY

What is an organization-wide negotiation strategy? In its most basic form it can be defined as "organizational agreement on negotiation guidelines and outcomes." In this context "organizational agreement" means the development of a consensus among all stakeholders in a company regarding how negotiations are to be conducted and what the results of those negotiations will be. These stakeholders include not just the field salesforce but also people in the legal department, product management, sales management, and even senior management.

Note that what the stakeholders must agree to are guidelines, not rules imposed on them by headquarters. Imposing centralized corporate constraints on negotiators in an effort to counter the effects of changes in the business world doesn't really solve the problem. In fact, when salespeople have to go through a pricing committee or some similar corporate group, the sales process becomes slow, bulky, inflexible, and non-customer-friendly. And it often results in losing sales to more creative competitors. At the other extreme, when salespeople are essentially allowed to do whatever they want, it invariably results in inconsistent customer and competitor messaging as well as inconsistent profits.

So even though having general agreement on a particular way to negotiate deals is beneficial to the entire organization, individual negotiators must have the flexibility to address their own situation as appropriate within those guidelines. Having a negotiation strategy developed by the appropriate stakeholders provides an organization with what we think of as a radically *centralized* strategy but radically *decentralized* execution. Once the stakeholders agree on ranges for what can be negotiated, they have the ability to move within those ranges and must go to management only in exceptional situations. And there are very few such exceptions when all of this is done right because of the creativity and flexibility built into the strategy.

But why should you establish such a negotiation strategy? There are several very good reasons, not the least of which is that it provides a means of successfully addressing the changes in the business environment that have made negotiation so much more difficult. When consensus exists in an organization about where you want to go in negotiations, how you're going to get there, and what the results will be, the result is inevitably a reduction in internal conflict and external variance. Reducing variance sends more proactive and consistent messages to both your customers and your competitors. And consistency enables you to avoid creating lack of trust in your customers and irrational behavior in your competitors. Ultimately, of course, the advantage of establishing a negotiation strategy is that these behavioral changes have a positive effect on the bottom line.

•   •   •   •   •

The process for designing and implementing an organization-wide negotiation strategy is essentially composed of five steps:

1. Identifying all the company's negotiation stakeholders
2. Training the stakeholders in the Strategic Negotiation Process
3. Writing the negotiation strategy
4. Distributing and implementing the strategy
5. Measuring the outcomes

Each of these steps takes from a few hours to a few days to accomplish, but once finished, you will have a complete process in place that will provide you with a considerable advantage over your competitors. Bear in mind, though, that the following is not intended as a comprehensive explanation of the process but, rather, an executive summary to give you a good general idea of how the process works.

Identifying All the Company's Negotiation Stakeholders

The key to establishing a successful negotiation strategy is stakeholder involvement. That's why the first step is determining all the members of the company's internal negotiation system. Again, this means not only the field salesforce but all those in the legal department as well as in sales, product, and senior management who are involved in negotiations. It's essential to include these groups for several reasons, perhaps the most important of which is that they all have their own particular roles in the process, their own methods, and their own interests in the outcome.

Salespeople, for example, are looking to make their quotas, while legal types are primarily interested in lowering risk. Sales managers are concerned with generating top-line sales revenues, while product managers are typically interested in the margins for their particular products. And senior management's most important priority is shareholder value. In addition to these unique concerns, these individuals are likely to have equally unique negotiation strategies and tactics. And unless those strategies and tactics are coordinated, the inevitable result is a great deal of internal misalignment and external confusion. All of this can be avoided, however, by involving them in the process. Involving them also has an additional benefit—it ultimately leads to a higher probability of adopting whatever strategy evolves from the process.

It's important to bear in mind that at this step it's not necessary to identify every single stakeholder. All you need to do is determine who all the stakeholders are and select a valid sample from each stakeholder group. If, for example, there are five lawyers, it's necessary to involve only one at this point. Similarly, if there are three salesforces—inside, regional, and national—that together amount to 1,500 salespeople, you need to choose only a few members from each of the salesforces to subsequently be involved in establishing a strategy.

Training the Stakeholders in the Strategic Negotiation Process

The next step in developing an organization-wide negotiation strategy is providing the individuals you selected to represent each of the stakeholder groups with training in the Strategic Negotiation Process. This may seem like an odd time to do this, but the timing is actually very important. Think about what you've just learned about blueprinting deals using the process. If you started talking to your sales manager about it tomorrow, would he or she understand what you were talking about? If you explained it really clearly, the sales manager might have a pretty good idea, but you'd still essentially be speaking what could just as easily be another language. If, though, your sales manager had read the book as well, he or she would have not only a complete understanding of the process, but also an appreciation of its benefits. Providing the stakeholders you've selected with this training will guarantee that they're all on the same page, and that they all understand both what needs to be done and why. In addition, our experience has shown that the two days we usually spend in this training tends to bind the participants together in a way that enables them to work more effectively as a group when they go on to the next step.

Writing the Negotiation Strategy

It's best to get to work on drafting a negotiation strategy as soon as possible after the stakeholders you've selected have gone through their training in the negotiation process and are still focused. Regardless of when they start, though, there are essentially three questions that they have to answer:

1. Why do we need a strategy?
2. How will we measure the results of the strategy once it's implemented?
3. What specific guidelines should be included in the strategy?

Why do we need a strategy? Step One is about the motivation for developing a strategy in the first place, the reason for making a change. It's been said that people don't change unless the pain of staying where they are is greater than the pain of changing. What you have to do at this point, then, is to make it clear to all those involved that, at least in this case, the cure is not worse than the disease. You do this by asking the stakeholders what kinds of problems they've encountered in the negotiation process. It's likely that they'll come up with a fairly long list, but it's best to pare the list down to the three to five most important issues. After going through this process, some of the answers companies typically arrive at include:

- Irrational competitor pricing is on the rise.
- There is too much internal negotiation, misalignment, and bureaucracy.
- Professional buyers are trying to make our product/service a commodity.
- We have margin pressure.
- Our sales process has us selling solutions, but we end up negotiating price.

No doubt you'll recognize that some of these problems are a result of the changes that have taken place in the negotiating environment. However, in many of the organizations in which we've been involved in this process, we've seen the effort to answer this question reveal that the real problem has nothing to do with negotiating. Rather, the real problem is the result of a nonexistent, broken, or poorly executed sales process. If, for example, salespeople are selling the wrong thing to the wrong buyers at the wrong level, developing a negotiation strategy—no matter how good—isn't going to even come close to eliminating the problem. And if the problem *is* in the sales process, it must be dealt with before any strategic negotiation initiative can be successful.

How will we measure the results of the strategy once it's implemented? Having determined why you need a strategy, the next step is to determine how you'll measure the results of that strategy after you've implemented it. The rationale behind determining outcomes first is that, by deciding where you want to go, you'll be in a better position to determine what actions you need to take in order to get there. We've found that the best way to express the desired outcomes is by establishing lagging indicators, and that, in doing so, there are three things you should bear in mind. First, to be useful to those negotiating deals on the street every day, you need to focus only on the most important negotiation issues, not all of them. Second, you have to remember that this is just about negotiation. There's a tendency during this process to bring up all sorts of business issues, whether they're service related, product related, or sales process related, and it's essential that you stay focused on negotiation. Finally, you have to be wary of including items that are extremely difficult, expensive, or time consuming to measure. It's all well and good to come up with great success measurements, but unless there is available benchmarking data on them, they're not going to do you much good.

An excellent way of establishing realistic lagging indicators is to say to yourself, "It's a year from now, our negotiation initiative has been very successful, and our results are as follows. . . ." But how do you fill in the rest of that sentence? Again, you do it by asking for input from your stakeholders. As with the question about why you need a strategy in the first place, the group will probably come up with a long list of answers. And like the answers to that question, it's best to focus on the three to five items that are most important in the negotiation process. In fact, once you have the list, a good way to pare it down is to ask your stakeholders to answer the following questions:

- What types of salespeople control the highest-margin deals?
- What types of customers generate the highest-margin deals?
- What are the 20 percent of deals that drive 80 percent of our revenues?

- What two or three things that adversely affect margins should we stop doing?
- What two or three things that positively affect margins should we do more of?
- What is our time frame for measuring these results?
- What aspects of the strategy are difficult and expensive to measure?
- What aspects of the strategy cannot be influenced in the negotiation process?

But there's also another good reason for paring down the list in this way. Our experience has shown that when you start implementing an organization-wide negotiation strategy, it's best to start small by using the process for only your highest-margin deals; and after you've achieved some success with it, extend your efforts to the entire organization. In other words, it should be evolution rather than revolution. Answering all these questions should provide you with a clearly targeted group of high-margin, high-profile deals to which you should start applying your negotiation strategy.

Some of the lagging indicators we've seen used by companies to measure the success of their negotiation strategies are the following:

- Discounts deeper than 10 percent will decrease from 30 percent of all deals to no more than 5 percent.
- Free licenses will decrease from 14 percent of all deals to zero.
- No request to reduce prices to match a competitor's will be considered until a full Consequences of No Agreement Estimation has been completed.
- Zero-sum concessions will decrease to zero in lieu of value-creating trades.
- The average customer satisfaction rating for negotiations for both internal and external customers will increase from 73 percent to 83 percent.

What specific guidelines should be included in the strategy?
Having determined why you should establish a negotiation strategy and the means by which you will measure its success, the third and final step in drafting the strategy is to decide exactly what guidelines it will include. The way to do this is to look at the lagging indicators you estab-

lished in the last step and again with the input of your stakeholders group, develop a specific action, or leading indicator, that will enable you to achieve it. Leading indicators can be divided into three groups: CNA related, Wish List related, and process related.

For example, one of the CNA-related lagging indicators I listed earlier was "No request to reduce prices to match a competitor's will be considered until a full Consequences of No Agreement Estimation has been completed." One way to achieve that would be to establish a leading indicator stating that "A negotiation process worksheet must be completed for any global account deal over $100,000."

Similarly, one of the Wish List–related lagging indicators I cited was "Free licenses will decrease from 14 percent of all deals to zero." A good way to address that problem might be to provide this leading indicator: "A request for a free license will be granted only when the customer is willing to trade something of equal value."

Finally, I mentioned this process-related lagging indicator: "The average customer satisfaction rating for negotiations for both internal and external customers will increase from 73 percent to 83 percent." Appropriate leading indicators to match this would be "All stakeholders will be trained in the negotiation process" or "For all global account deals over $100,000, multiple stakeholders will be involved in any negotiation planning prior to a customer meeting."

A complete negotiation strategy might then look like this:

Why Do We Need a Strategy?

- Irrational competitor pricing is on the rise.
- There is too much internal negotiation, misalignment, and bureaucracy.
- Professional buyers are trying to make our product/service a commodity.
- We have margin pressure.
- Our sales process has us selling solutions but we end up negotiating price.

What Specific Guidelines Should Be Included in the Strategy?

CNA-Related Guidelines
- A negotiation process worksheet must be completed for any global account over $100,000.

- We will conduct a review of a Consequences of No Agreement Estimation before reacting to irrational competitors.

Wish List–Related Guidelines
- We will not decrease our prices by 10 percent or more without trading for something of greater value.
- We will eliminate free licenses.
- We will include new service X in every negotiation.

Process-Related Guidelines
- All stakeholders will be trained in the negotiation process.
- For all global account deals over $100,000, multiple stakeholders will be involved in any negotiation planning prior to a customer meeting.

How Will We Measure the Results of the Strategy Once It's Implemented?

- No request to reduce prices to match competitors' prices will be considered until a full Consequences of No Agreement Estimation has been completed.
- Zero-sum concessions will decrease to zero in lieu of value-creating trades.
- Discounts deeper than 10 percent will decrease from 30 percent of all deals to no more than 5 percent.
- Free licenses will decrease from 14 percent of all deals to zero.
- The average customer satisfaction rating for negotiations for both internal and external customers will increase from 73 percent to 83 percent.

Distributing and Implementing the Strategy

Only after you have a version of a negotiation strategy that's satisfactory to all the stakeholders is it appropriate to start implementing that strategy. And the first step in that implementation is training your staff in the Strategic Negotiation Process that's the centerpiece of any successful strategy. By this point you will have already trained the sample group of stakeholders who were involved in developing the strategy, so this is when you extend the training to the rest of the staff. Again, though, it's important to note that by the word *staff* I don't mean only the field sales staff. Valuable as that training is, it can't in itself solve your negotiation problems. In fact, it's essential that everyone involved in negotiation in your organization be trained in how to blueprint deals—including sales management, product management, legal staff, and even senior staff—for two very good reasons. First, if only the field salesforce receives the training, its members will essentially wind up speaking a language different from the rest of your internal negotiation system. And, second, because those who haven't received the training won't really understand the process, they'll have little reason to reinforce the salespeople's new skills. As a result, it will be difficult, if not impossible, to make any real changes in your organization.

Of course, making changes in an organization, even under the best of circumstances, is always difficult. For that reason, as I mentioned earlier, even after you've had all the appropriate staff members trained, it's best to not move too quickly. You should start by using the process for only your most important deals, and then, after 6 to 12 months of success with them—once everyone in the organization can see how well it works—you can start applying the process to a wider sales audience and a wider range of negotiations. When you do, though, bear in mind that even at this point it may be necessary to revise your strategy. The competitive and customer landscape changes all the time, new products and services come and go, and a negotiation strategy must be fluid enough to take these changes into account. It may, in fact, be necessary to adjust your strategy as often as three to six times a year.

Even after all the appropriate staff have been trained, it's essential that you make sure that everyone knows about the strategy, understands it, and is capable of carrying it out. You can do this by both *auditing* and *coaching* your leaders and implementers. Auditing, of course, is just making sure that the strategy is being used to guide every new negotiation. Coaching is providing help to anyone who doesn't understand the strategy or process and is having trouble implementing it. Again, this is extremely important because by including everyone in your internal negotiating system in the process of defining the problems that need to be solved, determining how to solve those problems, and training to accomplish that end, you will substantially increase the likelihood of bringing about organizational change.

Measuring the Outcomes

The fifth and final step in establishing an organization-wide negotiation strategy is measuring the results. Of course, if you've taken all the previous steps correctly, the results should be exactly what you expected them to be. If, however, you find that despite your efforts you still haven't achieved the goals you set out earlier in the process, you need to go back and see what went wrong. It might, for example, be that you didn't properly identify all the company's stakeholders or you didn't determine reasonable and realistic goals. Our experience shows, however, that when goals aren't achieved, more often than not it's because the guidelines, the leading indicators, you established weren't followed. Correcting this may require additional auditing and/or coaching, but once you've provided those, you should find that you'll be able to consistently meet whatever goals you set for your organization.

A STRATEGY THAT INCREASES IN VALUE

One of the greatest benefits of establishing an organization-wide negotiation strategy is that, once established, it actually becomes increasingly more valuable to your organization. The reason is that it fosters both organization-wide knowledge and organization-wide cooperation on a scale undreamed of in most of today's companies. As already noted, fewer than 10 percent of all companies have a consistent and measured negotiation strategy and process. Because of that, in the vast majority of organizations every negotiation is seen as zero based and different from every other negotiation. But, as you now know, on a basic level all negotiations ultimately follow the same blueprint: Every negotiation entails perceived and real Consequences of No Agreement for both sides, as well as Wish Lists of items both sides want to obtain on reaching agreement. And when you have a negotiation strategy, and all your salespeople are tracking the negotiation process, few negotiations need be seen as either unprecedented or unusual because everyone in the organization has access to an enormous amount of invaluable data about previous deals, including:

- The most common customer Wish List items by both customer and product/service type

- The most common items your company asks for in return for these demands
- CNA Gap analysis by both customer and product/service type
- A library of CNA and Wish List questions used by everyone in the field
- A library of effective Multiple Equal Offers by customer and product/service type

Let's look, for example, at the first item on the list—the most common customer Wish List items. If you think of every negotiation as zero based, each time you have to negotiate with a new customer you're going to have to figure out what they're most likely to want. But imagine how much easier it would be for everyone in your organization if you've built up a database of information on your customers and know going in that the three demands you're most likely to encounter are 24/7 service, a three-year warranty, and free upgrades. Armed with that information, any salesperson in your organization will not only be able to understand the underlying reasons for these demands but, even more important, will be able to think through, in advance, multiple creative ways to address those reasons.

For example, one of our clients, a liquor distributor, tracked this data and found that the most common demand from both retail stores and bars/restaurants was for a reduction in price per case. But they also learned that the underlying reasons for these demands were different. The retail stores wanted lower prices because they wanted to offer cases at a discount as loss leaders to attract people into the stores and thus increase their margins. The bars/restaurants, on the other hand, wanted the discounts because it affected their cash flow and because they wanted to use that money for marketing. In response, instead of lowering its prices, the distributor created value for both sides by developing mutually beneficial programs to drive store traffic and improve margins for the retailer, as well as help bars/restaurants better regulate their cash flow and develop successful marketing programs. Most important, though, is that the distributor was able to do all this only because they had gathered the information about their customers and shared it among all their salespeople, which in turn enabled the salespeople to be ready with creative options when presented with those demands.

This is, of course, equally true for every aspect of the Strategic Negotiation Process. Having a library of information—whether it's about Wish List items, CNA or Wish List Estimations, or Multiple Equal Offers—enables you to anticipate, and prepare for, whatever demands your customers might make. Moreover, when this library has been established as a result of your developing both general agreement in your organization on where you want to go—your strategy, and how you're going to get there—and your process, you have a distinct and enormous advantage over your competitors.

A *p p e n d i x*

While the Strategic Negotiation Process is essentially an intellectual effort, recording the information you develop in written form is extremely helpful in successfully blueprinting deals. Not only does it help you organize all the data you gather during the process, but it enables you to see the blueprint in its entirety at a glance once it's completed.

For that reason, we have developed the following Strategic Negotiation Worksheet. The first sample of the worksheet has been completed using the data from the second case study in Chapter 11. Following that is a one-page instruction sheet for completing the worksheet, and a blank worksheet you can use for the information gathered for your own negotiation.

Please note that the worksheets are copyrighted material and are not to be copied.

Strategic Negotiation Worksheet

Goal for the Negotiation: _Create joint value and divide it given concerns for fairness in the ongoing relationship._

Section 1: Consequences of No Agreement

Our Side		The Other Side	
CNA: _Lose the business_	Not sure ___	CNA: _Go to competitor: Operations Consulting_	Not sure ___
Quantitative: _Lose $750k - $2.5m in sales (−)_	Not sure ___	Quantitative: _Have to pay for customization (−)_	Not sure ___
Lose $25k in sales-related costs (−)		_Less reliable machines (−)_	
May impact my bonus $ (−)		_Lower up-front costs (+)_	
Have to replace with many deals (−)		_Higher cost of ownership (−)_	
Qualitative: _Political heat from VP Global Sales (−)_	Not sure ___	Qualitative: _Customer will be big fish in small pond (+)_	Not sure ___
Pressure from Product Management (−)			
Might be easy to replace this sale (+)			

Based on what you know, who has more power?   Us ___   Them __X__   Not sure ___

Has the other side correctly diagnosed their CNA?   Yes ___   No __X__   Not sure ___

Section 2: Developing Wish Lists

Main item for us	Range		Main item for them	Range
1. Contract length - 30%	3 – 1 years		1. Price – 40%	$200-$300k/machine
Other items	**Range**		**Other items**	**Range**
2. Price – 25%	$300-$250k/machine		2. Ongoing Service – 25%	24x7 – 8x5
3. Volume – 15%	3-2 machines		3. Upgrades – 15%	Free-75% discount
4. Upgrades – 15%	50% discount-free		4. Contract length – 10%	1-? Years
5. Man hours provided – 10%	100-150		5. Volume – 5%	2 machines-?
6. Ongoing service – 5%	8x5 – 24/7		6. Man hours – 5%	200-100

(1 = top priority   6 = lowest priority)   (1 = top priority   6 = lowest priority)

Broaden the negotiation: (Things we want that they have)
- _Business in other countries?_
-
-

Broaden the negotiation: (Things we have that they may want)
- _Access to our thought leaders?_
-
-

Section 3: Preparing to Validate the Estimation

Data we need on:

Their CNA	**How we get the data:**	List CNA questions to ask the other side
• How they see it	List public data sources	• How much customization is needed?
	• Lexus-Nexus search	• How much impact/time during installation?
	• Industry reports	• Expectations in terms of machine downtime?
	•	• How much service do you expect?
	•	• How much staff training do you need?
	•	• Budget for maintenance years 1-4?

Their prioritized Wish List		Wish List questions to ask the other side
• Do we have the right trades in mind?	Not available publicly for trades	• What is missing or should be deleted from my list?
• How are they prioritized and weighted?		• What would you rank as lead priority?
•		• How about 2nd, 3rd, and 4th?
•		• Do you have specific targets for each?
•		• How important is Number 1 (weighting)?
		•

Section 4: Validation

Validation call date: 10/2   People to invite: _VP Mfg_   _VP Sourcing_   _CFO_

Section 5: Creating MEOs: Bundled Relationships / Offers (based on both sides' CNAs/prioritized trades)

Title: Short term – low price	**Title:** Long term and strategic	**Title:** A middle ground
One-year contract	Three-year contract	Two-year contract
$295k/machine	$250k/machine	$275k/machine
One machine	Three machines	Two machines
Service: 8 hours x 5 days	Service: 24 hours x 7 days	Service: 24 hours x 5 days
Upgrades: Free	Upgrades: Free	Upgrades: 75% discount
Install support: 100 hours	Install support: 300 hours	Install support: 200 hours

Section 6: Presenting MEOs

Presentation date: _11/1_   People to invite: _VP Mfg_   _VP Sourcing_   _CFO_   Rehearse date: _____

How to Complete the Strategic Negotiation Worksheet

Section 1: Your CNA, Left Side	Section 1: Their CNA, Right Side
To complete this section, answer these questions: • **CNA** – If you don't reach agreement with the other side, what will the ramifications be? • **Quantitative** – What are the measurable "hard costs or benefits" to you of losing this deal? • **Qualitative** – What are the "soft costs or benefits" to you of losing this deal, e.g., hassle, politics?	To complete this section, answer these questions: • **CNA** – If the other side doesn't reach agreement with you on this negotiation, what will they do as an alternative? • **Quantitative** – What are the measurable "hard costs or benefits" of that alternative versus your offer? • **Qualitative** – What are the "soft costs or benefits" of that alternative versus your offer, e.g., hassle, politics?

Section 2: Developing Wish Lists

Main Item – How would both sides define the main item of this negotiation? Many times this is the same for both sides. Items like price and right to use are typical as main issues of a negotiation. How many of these things does each side want?

Other Wish List Items – Beyond the main item, what other items make this a great deal? Many times these are the same for both your side and theirs (although they often differ in terms of their importance to each side). Volume, length of contract, compliance, contract terms, and billing terms are typical Wish List items.

Broaden the Negotiation – Beyond the main and other Wish List items, these are items that are not typically defined as part of the negotiation. These may include such things as access to their "thought leaders" or the ability to expand the relationship globally.

Section 3: Preparing to Validate the Estimations

Data you need on their CNA and Wish List items, ranking, and weighting – In sections 1 and 2 you used your own knowledge, that of coworkers, and publicly available data to estimate their CNA and Wish List. Now you need to challenge your own estimation and list data you are missing or have guessed at.	**Data sources and questions** – Use 10K forms, annual reports, Web pages, Internet searches, Lexus-Nexus article searches, and any other publicly available data to learn more about the other side. Find people in your organization, the other side's organization, and outside both that can help "fill in the blanks." Once you've used all other data sources, prepare specific questions to ask the other side to verify your estimations and determine where you have miscalculated.

Section 4: Validation

In doing your scheduling, remember to position the call/visit as a "needs analysis." Remember the 80/20 listening rule and avoid "doing the deal" at the validation meeting, unless the other side offers a deal strikingly better than your CNA. Invite all appropriate members of the other side's team and bring appropriate members from your side.

Section 5: Creating MEOs

Use the work you did in diagnosing both sides' CNA and Wish Lists to develop your MEOs. Include as many trades as possible that speak to the needs of both sides and exceed CNAs. Have the other side rank MEOs as most to least desirable. Be sure to title each MEO.

Section 6: Presenting MEOs

Invite all appropriate management levels from both sides. Use this meeting as an opportunity to continue manipulating MEOs to create additional joint value.

Strategic Negotiation Worksheet

Goal for the Negotiation: *Create joint value and divide it given concerns for fairness in the ongoing relationship.*

Section 1: Consequences of No Agreement

	Our Side		The Other Side
CNA:		CNA:	
Quantitative	_____ Not sure ___	Quantitative	_____ Not sure ___
Quantitative	_____ Not sure ___		
Qualitative	_____ Not sure ___	Qualitative	_____ Not sure ___

Based on what you know, who has more power? Us ___ Them ___

Has the other side correctly diagnosed their CNA? Yes ___ No ___ Not sure ___

Section 2: Developing Wish Lists

Our Side		The Other Side	
Main item for us	Range	Main item for them	Range
1.		1.	
Other items	Range	Other items	Range
2.		2.	
3.		3.	
4.		4.	
5.		5.	
6.		6.	

(1 = top priority   6 = lowest priority)

Broaden the negotiation: (Things we want that they have)

•
•
•

(1 = top priority   6 = lowest priority)

Broaden the negotiation: (Things we have that they may want), estimate

•
•
•

Section 3: Preparing to Validate the Estimation

Data we need on:

How we get the data:

Their CNA	List public data sources	List CNA questions to ask the other side
•	•	•
•	•	•
•	•	•
•	•	•
•	•	•

Their prioritized Wish List		Wish List questions to ask the other side
•		•
•		•
•		•
•		•
•		•

Section 4: Validation

Validation call date: _____   People to invite: _____

Section 5: Creating MEOs: Bundled Relationships / Offers (based on both sides' CNAs/prioritized trades)

Title: _____   Title: _____   Title: _____

Section 6: Presenting MEOs

Presentation date: _____   People to invite: _____   Rehearse date: _____

Share the message!

Bulk discounts
Discounts start at only 10 copies. Save up to 55% off retail price.

Custom publishing
Private label a cover with your organization's name and logo. Or, tailor information to your needs with a custom pamphlet that highlights specific chapters.

Ancillaries
Workshop outlines, videos, and other products are available on select titles.

Dynamic speakers
Engaging authors are available to share their expertise and insight at your event.

Call Dearborn Trade Special Sales at 1-800-245-BOOK (2665)
or e-mail trade@dearborn.com